PRODUCTIVITY DRIVEN SUCCESS

HIDDEN SECRETS OF ORGANIZATIONAL EFFICIENCY

ERIC P. BLOOM

Productivity Driven Success

Aviva Publishing
Lake Placid, NY
518-523-1320
www.avivapubs.com

ISBN: 978-1-947937-88-8
Library of Congress Number: 2020908164

Every attempt has been made to source properly all quotes.
Printed in the United States of America

CONTENTS

To Juliette Marie Bloom, the newest addition to the Bloom family:

In addition to being a beautiful bundle of cuteness and joy, with your first breath, I become a grandfather, my son and daughter-in-law, Jonathan and Jeannie became parents, and a new family came into being.

Welcome to the world and welcome to our family!

Love,

Grandpa

ACKNOWLEDGEMENTS

———————

This book has been thirty years in the making. Over the years as an individual contributor, manager, corporate executive, and entrepreneur, I've been given great advice on how to improve the productivity of the teams I've led and the productivity of my company, Manager Mechanics. To all those who have been kind enough to share their knowledge, thank you. I have honored you by helping those I've managed and to those I've mentored within this book. To quote Father James Keller, "A candle never loses it light when it lights another candle."

I would also like to thank those in my Book Support Group, a group of people I trust and respect, who were kind enough to find the time to review this manuscript before it was sent to my publisher. Your input was greatly appreciated and truly enhanced the book's quality, thoughtfulness, and completeness. Through your advice, chapters were added, superfluous information was removed, descriptions were enhanced and key concepts were further clarified. Your thoughts were heeded and incorporated within this book. In particular, I would like to thank Amy Wallace, Tom Catalini, Jon Rider, Steve Balzac, Patrick O'Malley, Linda Varone, Peter Ward, and Eric Cole for going above and beyond with their incredible help and advice.

I was also given an enormous amount of professional advice and would like to thank Henry Devries, Mark LeBlanc and Marilee Driscoll for their wit, wisdom, and guidance.

Lastly, I would like to thank Justin Sachs, the owner of Motivational Press, for his support, trust, and his willingness to publish this book. Thank you.

Turing from friends and colleagues to family, I would like to thank the best proofreading team on planet earth, my parents. Your great editing aside, the pleasure of working with you on this endeavor goes beyond words. Thanks for being my proofreaders of everything written and my mentors in life. I love you both. Also thanks to my wife Cheryl, who has patiently listened to me talk about this book for months. Your advice, support, and unique perspective have been of great value to me as both an author and a person. My love and thanks to you also.

PRODUCTIVITY DRIVEN SUCCESS

Hidden Secrets of Organizational Efficiency

· · · · ·

» Many-to-many interaction

» Email

9. Time Management: Spending Time Like It's Money

» Protect Your Schedule Using "Near-Time Far-Time"

» Physical exercise Can Help Improve Your Productivity

» Spending Time "on" and "in" Your Department

» Planned Multi-Tasking Enhances Throughput

» Required Work vs. Requested Work

» Ten Places to Find Department Productivity Killers

» Ten Things Your Department Can Do During Slow Times

10. Leveraging the Zone: Magnifying Your Creativity and Output

» What is "Being in the Zone?"

» Maximize Productivity by Using Zone Level Prioritization

» Management Time vs. Worker Time

» Don't Mix Operational and Non-Operational Tasks

» Meeting Times Based on Circadian Rhythms

» Working in the Shower Can be Very Productive

11. Ongoing Process Improvement: Discovering Small Gains That Make Big Wins

» Decide which process to enhance

» Measure the current factors you wish to improve (i.e. time, cost, etc.)

» Enhance the process

» Re-measure the factors you tried to improve

» Report the value of the process enhancement

12. Asset Reuse: Solving the puzzle of buying/building it once and using it again and again

» Create an asset inventory

» Categorize and combine assets into logical groups

» Assess asset reuse potential

» Identify potential reuse partners

» Gain approval

» Implement reuse plan

» Measure results

13. Knowledge Storage and Transfer: Organizational learning at its best

» Knowledge Creation

» Knowledge Retention

» Knowledge Distribution

PART 3 – Structuring Your Productivity Approach

14. Operationalizing the Pyramid

15. Productivity Linking and Mapping

16. Getting your Productivity Projects Funded

PART 4 - Productivity Superstars

17. CEO has Thinning Profit Margins

18. After Year of IT Budget Cuts, CIO Gets Growth

19. SVP of Sales Hires a Consultant

20. SVP of Human Resources Leads the Charge

PREFACE

Becoming a Productivity Superstar

• • • • •

What is your story? Better still, what could your story become?

Whether you are an individual contributor, a senior executive, or a sole entrepreneur, productivity enhancement can help you and your company move forward.

As you read this book, you'll find many concepts, processes, and techniques to enhance your organization's productivity. Do not try to implement them all. There are far too many to implement and some will not be applicable to your organization. The trick to using this book effectively is like finding gold in a mountain. Sift away what doesn't currently meet your business needs to reveal the real nuggets of gold that can help drive your professional career and your company forward.

This book is divided into four parts: Part 1 provides a conceptual framework for organizational productivity in general. It begins by defining the opportunity cost of poor organizational productivity. Next, it describes how maximizing my company's productivity created many of the conceptual underpinnings for this book. It then changes gears. The next chapter describes the seven steps of the "Productivity Pyramid," which simultaneously describes the building blocks of a mature productivity-based organization as well as illuminate the steppingstones toward organizational efficiency. The last chapter in this section outlines the importance of having a productivity-oriented culture and how to create one.

Part 2 describes eight "Productivity Amplifiers". In essence, these eight categories of techniques are designed to enhance some aspect of organizational efficiency. Hidden within these category names is an acronym that gives light to the book's original name. The first letter of each category spells the word "cocktail". The book's original name was "Productivity Cocktail".

Part 3 outlines the Productivity Pyramid System (PPS) and provides suggestions on how to get your projects funded. PPS is a seven step process designed to maximize the effectiveness and value of your productivity initiatives. The chapter "Getting your Productivity Projects Funded" describes how to incorporate your initiatives into your organization's existing project definition, approval, prioritization and funding processes. All too often, productivity-related projects are done on their own, separated from the mainstream activities. This segregation reduces their legitimacy and reduces their chance of success.

Part 4 explains how these techniques described in the book can be used practically.

Lastly, from writer to reader, I hope you find this book valuable and that the concepts within it will help guide your organization toward the time, money, and resources it needs to do truly great things. If you succeed, your company's story will become your own, making you a productivity superstar.

PART 1

VISUALIZE THE BIG PICTURE

1. IGNITING YOUR PRODUCTIVITY CULTURE ENABLERS

Concentrate all your thoughts upon the work in hand.
The sun's rays do not burn until brought to a focus.

— Alexander Graham Bell

As people have personalities, organizations have cultures. Some people are open to change and some are not. Some organizations embrace change as a catalyst for future growth and profitability, while some do not. Make no mistake, increasing your productivity requires change. If your organization views change as an important business attribute, then ongoing productivity improvement will be the status quo. If your company is set in its ways, refuses to streamline its processes and shuns innovation, then productivity improvement is not required. Given today's business environment, the company will soon stagger under its own weight and fade away. That being said, if you are working at this type of firm, the best way for you to be productive is by updating your resume.

Over the course of my professional life, I've seen many great companies, small and large, get too set in their ways because of their incredible success. When new technologies or

> *"As people have personalities, organizations have cultures"*

more advanced products came along, these companies either couldn't, or wouldn't embrace the new industry directions. They eventually became a shell of their former greatness, where they were either bought out and merged, or simply went out of business. I always found this difficult to watch, not only because it's always hard to see a success story fade, but also because of the talented people they left unemployed in their declining wake.

Six organizational attributes can give your organizations the ability to define, accept, and implement both small and large changes that productivity enhancements require. These attributes are:

1. Cultural Awareness
2. Innovative Mindset
3. Management Focus
4. Employee Communication
5. Self and Organizational Learning
6. Conflict Avoidance and Resolution

1. Cultural Awareness: ("Culture Eats Strategy for Breakfast")

One of the most important business attributes is cultural awareness, or the ability to understand your organization's internal politics, idiosyncrasies, strengths and weaknesses, and how it gets things done. To make matters more complicated, organizations have multiple subcultures. For example, the Sales department may have a different internal culture versus the Internal Accounting. The corporate headquarters in Boston may have a very different culture than the satellite offices in Chicago, or London. Therefore, your productivity initiative may be very successful in the Boston office, but fail miserably in Chicago, or London.

I first witnessed this subculture phenomenon very early in my career, while I was working for a large computer manufacturer. I was a computer programmer working to automate the general ledger portion of their accounting system. I worked with people from the Accounting, Sales, and Manufacturing groups. I actually kept three sets of clothes in my car. The accountants dressed

> "To make matters more complicated, organizations have multiple cultures, called subcultures."

business casual. The sales people wore suits and the manufacturing people wore jeans and t-shirts. If I visited a group wearing the wrong clothing, they wouldn't take me seriously. Given it was a large company, these three organizational areas luckily were housed in different buildings. So, I actually kept three sets of clothes in my car and found myself continually changing my clothes in local restaurants, or my car, as I went from business unit to business unit. Perhaps if I'd been older or more experienced, it wouldn't have been an issue. However, my point is that the perceptions and biases of each subculture had to be recognized and taken into account if I wanted to succeed.

Before moving forward with a productivity initiative, you must first ask yourself: "Does this operational change require cultural change first?" The answer may depend on whether the proposed changes are aligned and consistent with the current organizational culture.

Peter Drucker was known for saying: "Culture eats strategy for breakfast." The idea behind this is that you can define a great strategy, but it isn't consistent with your organization's cultural norms, then it will most likely fail. You must take your organization's culture into account when selecting which project to undertake. For example, if your company's culture believes that all work should be done physically at the office, a productivity initiative that includes allowing people to work from home will be difficult, if not impossible to implement. Once a project is selected, it must also be designed and implemented in a culturally appropriate way. For example, if the company is very email laden from adding too many unneeded people on each email, you must first change the cultural belief that this is of value, before implementing procedural steps, such as removing the "Reply All" button from the email input screen.

2. Innovative Mindset: (Think Different to Solve Problems)

Opportunities to innovatively enhance productivity come in many forms. It could be successful creation, implementation, reuse and/or improvement of an existing business process. It could be sales technique, or cultural factor that reduces costs, which enhances productivity, increases company competitiveness, or provides other business value.

Finding these innovative solutions requires a willingness to look at your existing processes with a critical eye, even if you were the one who originally designed them. Albert Einstein had a quote saying that: "No problem can be solved from the same level of consciousness that created it." That is to say, you must think about your processes from new perspectives in order to improve them. I bring this up for two reasons: first, to encourage you and your staff to be willing to think outside-the-box and have the courage to look at old issues in new ways; second, given the fact that this is a book on productivity, efficiency, and innovation, it should have at least one Albert Einstein quote to make it official.

There are ten questions you can ask yourself that may help you drive innovation within your organization, even if it's is only you:

1. How are other industries using technologies that my company currently owns?
2. What technologies are my competitors using that are giving them an edge against my company?
3. How can I combine two, or more, of the same technologies that my company owns to solve business problems in creative ways?
4. What open source software can be inexpensively and securely added to our list of tools that helps organizational productivity?

5. If budget was not an issue, what could I do to improve/enhance my technical environment? How can I do it less expensively?

6. Are there any business processes that could/should be done more efficiently? If so, how?

7. What technologies are we currently using that should be phased out to make budget dollars available for new innovative initiatives?

8. What can I personally do to help foster an innovative company culture? Can it be started today?

9. What measurements can I use to show the return on investment of my innovative ideas?

10. If I knew I would not fail, what innovation would I try to implement at my company? Then, is there a way I can minimize the risk of failure on the project?

My next challenge to you is to expand on this list based on your job, your technical profession, your job level, your areas of ability, and your areas of interest. Then ask yourself these questions continuously. With a little luck and a great idea, you can make an incredible contribution to your company, and in turn, your own professional future.

A number of years ago, I headed up the IT group of a financial services firm. We had a computer program running nightly that analyzed the portfolio performance impact of each stock and bond held within each portfolio. This program ran for almost five hours each evening. It was very well written and accurate. However, it took too long to run. For those in the asset management business, it was a portfolio attribution program.

I hired a person with a very strong mathematical background and light programming experience to analyze this portfolio attribution program to see if he could discover a way for it to run more quickly.

My thought was that it would expose him to professional quality software development practices. About two weeks later, he came into my office and said the program could now be run in five minutes. Given his newness to the profession, the complexity of the software, and the enormous amount of data chugging the program required, my first thought was that he had made a mistake that skipped major portions of the software from running. However, the program actually did run in five minutes. Given his strong math background, he was able to define a more efficient algorithm to perform the calculations.

> "The diversity of thought created by hiring a wide variety of people brings new problem solving perspectives to an issue."

The point I'm making is that diversity brings innovation. What was outside the box thinking for the computer programmers, was inside the box thinking for a mathematician. By nature, the diversity of thought created by hiring a wide variety of people brings new problem solving perspectives to an issue. My suggestion is to embrace diversity of all types in your hiring practices because it will facilitate an innovative mindset.

3. MANAGEMENT FOCUS: (SENIOR LEADERSHIP IS REQUIRED)

All organizational initiatives must have management support. If not, then they probably will not get funded. If they do, they will wither on the vine. If you are the project's executive champion, then great. However, if you are not the executive in charge, then you must find one who can provide you with the resources and political clout needed to move you from an idea to an ongoing business practice.

If an executive of this type cannot be found, then it may be worthwhile to move inward and ask yourself the following questions:

1. If implemented, can my idea actually provide the productivity gains I'm proposing?

2. Is my idea consistent with the organization's culture?

3. Does the company have the financial resources to fund productivity improvement initiatives?

4. Is my idea consistent with the company's future direction, goals, and objectives?

5. Did I present my idea to senior management in the best possible light?

6. Is it a great idea that should be proposed again at a later date when the company has more time, money and/or other resources to give it the priority it deserves?

Over the years, I have worked on projects that for one reason, or another, were not favored by senior management. It was always an uphill battle to get resources, cooperation from other groups, and/or recognition for our hard work. If your productivity projects are not favored by your leadership, even if they are initially funded, then their effect will most likely not be long lasting.

4. EMPLOYEE COMMUNICATION: (CLARITY, CONSISTENCY AND HUMAN CONNECTION)

Remember that virtually all productivity enhancements are a form of change; therefore, the change must be communicated to those affected by it in the following ways:

» Be clear about what you want to say.

» Be consistent in your messaging.

» Be aware that varying audiences have different needs and worries.

» Explain rationale that is relatable to the issue.

» People are persuaded more by human dimension than statistical facts.

» Your genuine passion and enthusiasm can activate similar feelings in your listeners.

Each of these communication tru-isms views employee communication from a different perspective:

> *"Productivity enhancements are a form of change; therefore, the change must be communicated to those affected."*

Be clear about what you want to say

If you are not clear in your own mind as to what you have to say and how you want to say it, it will come across as either insincere or unclear about the goal you are trying to achieve. Neither of these will gain employee support and/or motivation.

Be consistent in your messaging

If you are consistently changing the reason, process, or expected outcome of your proposed productivity gain, then it will confuse those you are trying to convince. In turn, this confusion will reduce their motivation to provide assistance and worse, cause them to believe you have a hidden motive that isn't being communicated. When suspicious, people tend to think the worst. They begin to fear that it could be reductions in staff, or outsourcing. If people believe this, they will fight your productivity initiative at every step. People have a hard time understanding a concept that will reduce their pay.

Be aware that varying audiences have different needs and worries

This statement basically means that you must know your audience. For example, you wish to implement new software that will make the Finance Department more efficient. If you present this software enhancement to the Finance staff by saying it will make them so efficient that half of them will be losing their jobs, then it will be problematic to gain their support. Alternatively, if you say this new software will increase the amount of time they have to service their internal clients and perform advanced financial analytics, they will be much more likely to adopt the new software platform.

Explain rationale in a way that listeners can best relate

Here you must also know your audience, but from a different perspective. In this case, you must present your message in a way they will best understand. If you are speaking to the Accounting Department, craft your message from an accountant's perspective; when you are speaking with the Human Resource department, use HR terminology. Of course, it must be the same message, just delivered slightly different based on the listeners' lexicon and point of view.

People are persuaded more by human dimension than statistical facts

Tell a story; don't just use facts and figures. People have been using storytelling as a form of communication for thousands of years. The reason for its longevity is because it works so well.As the expression goes, "if it isn't broke, don't fix it."

Your genuine passion and enthusiasm can create similar feeling in your listeners

Lastly, if you are not passionate about what you are trying to do, then why should anyone else? The best way for you to motivate others is to first be motivated yourself. When you are truly motivated with the goal you are trying to achieve, then people will innately feel your energy. That's why people love to be near entrepreneurs who are passionate about their companies. Their passion and energy are infectious.

As described above, communication is an essential part of productivity based change. It's also a key component of good management. Regardless of profession or topic, I have found communication with my staff, peers, boss, and clients/customers was the right thing to do. As managers, we have two functions: communication and decision making. Productivity projects aside, properly communicating with others and making good managerial decisions can easily become your most effective productivity driver by enhancing employee morale, reducing attrition, and fostering employee empowerment.

5. Self and Organizational Learning: (Advancement Through Acquiring Business and Leadership Skills)

For an organization to grow, it must continue to learn. This acquired knowledge, whether through formal training, or business experience, provides insights that facilitate growth and improved processes. Personal learning greatly enhances your ability to think outside the box because you can do so from a position of enhanced knowledge, combined with innate cleverness.

Organizational learning is also developed through a combination of formalized education and business experience, both of which are driven (or suppressed) by the organization's culture. Different employees need different types of training in order to grow. Technologists need to learn new technologies. Senior executives need to keep abreast of industry trends and corporate practices; therefore, all employees need to maximize their interpersonal skills, business skills, and emotional intelligence.

Professional curiosity in both individuals and organizations causes them to be both introspective and more aware of their external environment. Introspection causes people to ask the

> *"Different employees need different types of training in order to grow."*

question: "How can I improve?" External awareness causes people to ask "What can I learn from my surroundings that can help me and/or my company successfully move forward?" Both of these questions lead to innovative thought and drive productivity.

I didn't truly understand the importance of training until I started a training company specializing in leadership, soft/business, and productivity skills. I'm not saying this as a way to bolster my industry. I'm saying this because I believe if I had taken this type of training more seriously earlier in my professional life, then it would have moved my career forward more quickly/easily. As a technical professional by education and background, I discounted the importance of such skills because of my technical abilities. Yes, my technical abilities opened the door to my managerial career, but it wasn't until my business and leadership skills evolved that I was able to move into the senior managerial ranks.

6. CONFLICT PREVENTION AND RESOLUTION: (5 CAUSES OF CONFLICT)

In short, productivity drives change and change drives conflict. The ability to minimize this conflict helps facilitate change, which in turn, drives productivity. Your personal and organizational ability to deal effectively with conflict can make, or break your ability to enhance organizational productivity.

Work done by Christopher Moore suggests that all conflict is caused by five factors:

» Data: Information is lacking, differently interpreted or withheld

» Interest: There are scarce resources, such as money or skilled workers

» Value: Different ways of life, deeply rooted goals or varying criteria on how to evaluate behaviors

» Relationship: Strong emotions, stereotypes, and/or poor communication

» Structural: Inequities in control, ownership, power, authority or geographic separation.

Certainly, conflict resolution can easily be a full book by itself. I'll simply say here that if you identify the reasons causing the conflict, then it will make it easier for you to solve and move your project forward.

A good thing to remember: if your project is being slowed or stopped by someone remember that 99% of the time people are not against you, they are for themselves. If you can understand the reason behind their objections, then you can very often turn enemies into allies.

Next time you are having an issue with a fellow employee impeding your project's progress, give this concept a try. Attempt to analyze the reason he/she is blocking your way. Then try to gain their support by explaining how your project's success has value to him/her professionally.

Ending thought

Whether you are a CEO or the newest college intern, being the agent of change that enhances your organization's productivity will be of great value to your organization and has the potential to bring your career to new heights.

2. THEORIZING ORGANIZATIONAL PRODUCTIVITY

What you do today can improve all your tomorrow.

— Anonymous

The majority of this book contains a combination of practical concepts, tips, tricks and techniques designed to help you maximize your organization's productivity. This chapter is designed to give you a basic understanding of what productivity is, how you can enhance it, how you can measure it, and the value it brings to your organization.

Organizational productivity is generally defined by using the following formula:

Productivity = Output / Input

This formula by itself, however, provides no real value. To be useful, you must consider:

» What type of productivity are you trying to measure?

» What is the optimal output you wish to achieve?

» Can the expended inputs be better used on other initiatives?

» Are the productivity measures you are calculating getting better or worse?

» How does your productivity and cost structure compare to your competitors?

» Does this level of productivity help you meet your organizational goals?

Moving this productivity value mathematically can be done in various ways as shown below:

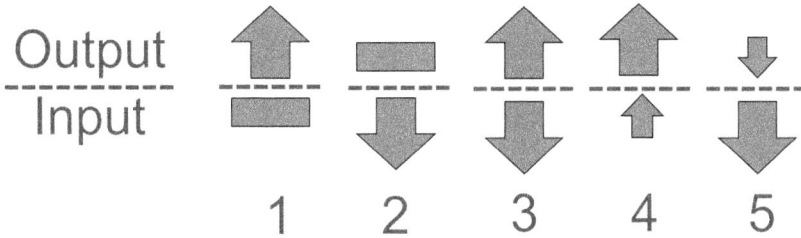

$$\frac{Output}{Input}$$

1   2   3   4   5

In the first scenario, output increases without a corresponding increase in input. This type of situation can occur by reducing waste or by using existing outputs in new ways that provide additional value. The second occurs via process improvement or other reductions in costs. The third scenario is the best, when outputs are increased and inputs are decreased. This usually happens through computer automation, the purchase of physical devices or the redesign of a poorly designed process. The fourth way is produced when modifying the inputs provide a disproportionate amount of value. It also can be produced through economies of scale, namely, as volume increases, processes gain efficiency. Lastly, in the fifth circumstance a large reduction in input can produce a disproportionately small reduction in output. This is often created when a process was initially overstaffed and/or over-automated in anticipation of higher volumes which never materialized.

Over the course of my career, I have had the benefit of seeing all five of these scenarios. Unfortunately, I have also seen the reverse, where productivity has fallen, rather than enhanced. In most cases it was not that the inputs have been reduced, except in bad economic times or through organizational realignment, it was because of bad internal company politics, seemingly good decisions with unexpected results, poor employee morale, miscommunication, mergers that went awry, or a lack of management attention. All of these productivity gains or losses were always caused by positive or negative changes to the inputs and outputs of this simple formula.

This brings us to our next question, what are these inputs and outputs? Typical inputs include:

» Mental energy: By senior management, individual contributors, contactors/consultants, and/or vendors

» Work time: By employees of all types, contractors and all others on your behalf

» Money: Expense of all types, including hourly employee costs

» Resources: Of all types, including physical devices like computers and trucks, as well as all consumable-type items

» Risk: New processes and projects of types contain an element of risk that should not be overlooked

The outputs related to this equation are, of course, whatever you are trying to produce, but generically they can be described as:

» Reduced work time

» Money

» Freed up resources

» Increased quality

» Reduced risk

» Shorter delivery times

» Enhanced employee culture

» Corporate growth

Moving from the conceptual to the actual, the definition of productivity improvement must be holistic in nature and allow you to receive multiple benefits from the same action, repurpose internal assets at no additional cost, stop doing things that don't need to be done, do things faster, and/or get things at lower cost in a way that provides re-investable time, money and/or resources that can be used to enhance the organization. This should all be done while maintaining or decreasing risk maintaining or increasing quality, using proper business ethics and maintaining your peace of mind.

Compare the above lists of inputs and outputs to the actual inputs used in the processes and tasks your team performs. This knowledge is the first step toward insights as to how these inputs can be used to provide great output or reduce. It can also provide ideas related to streamlining your existing processes.

Also, for your organizational productivity improvements to be effective and long lasting, they cannot be randomly performed, they must be:

» Aligned to organizational goals and objectives

» Holistic in nature, regarding analyzing all potential productivity options, selecting the mix that best supports organizational ob-jectives, provides needed productivity gains, and doesn't cause productivity reducing side effects

» Systematic through the creation and execution of formalized project plans and project management best practices

» Measurable to illustrate tangible business benefits

» Profitable by providing additional time, money and resources back to the organization toward meeting organizational goals

No one is really interested in productivity, what they are truly interested in are the time, money and resources it generates, the business models it creates, the competitive advantages it provides, the corporate growth it generates and the ability to simply get more things done.

Using the opportunity that productivity provides is the key to taking advantage or your organizational productivity initiatives.

3. CAPTURING LOST OPPORTUNITY COST

The four most dangerous words in investing are: 'This time it's different.'

- Sir John Templeton

What could your organization do today if it had more time, money, or even resources to get things done? This is what enhanced productivity can do for you.

For example, if you have five people working toward the completion of a specified task and can find a way to complete it using only four people, you can have the fifth person working on something else. Let's say these same five people are contractors, not employees, making $50 per hour; therefore, if the project is three weeks long, then the reduction of one contractor saves $6,000 ($50 per hour X 40 hours per week X 3 weeks). As a manager, you can allocate that money towards a different project, use it to purchase other goods and services, or simply come in under budget and make your boss happy. The cost of poor productivity is the lost opportunity to do other things.

Let's look again at how that $6,000 productivity can be repurposed within a business. It could be used to help increase revenue by spending it to optimize the company website. Another use would be to hire a college intern at $15 for an entire summer ($6000 / $15 per hour / 40 hours per week = 10 weeks). Just imagine how much work a college intern could do for you in just ten weeks! Alternatively, that $6,000 could also be used to purchase a needed piece of software, such as a new budgeting application, that could increase the productivity of the Finance Department by 10% for an estimated five year period. "10% X 5 years" is quite a bit of savings that can; in turn, be used to fund other productivity enhancements, and the cycle continues.

Looking back to the previous example, if you had not found a way to use four contactors instead of five, you could not have purchased the software needed to improve the productivity of the Finance Department. The name for this lost opportunity is "Opportunity Cost".

What is your opportunity cost of low organizational productivity? What could your organization do today if it had more time, money, or resources to get things done? Is it increased revenue, improved profitability, more customers, work/life balance, or some other goal? All these aspirations have one thing in common; the need for time, money, or resources to make them happen.

This concept of using enhanced productivity as a way to fund other activities is as true for large corporations as it is for an individual employee. The only differences are the complexity of the issues, the size of the opportunity costs, and the

> *"What could your organization do today if it had more time, money, or resources to get things done?"*

size of the benefits to be realized. The collective opportunity cost of hundreds, thousands, or tens of thousands of dollars spent on operational inefficiencies are like the sand running through an hourglass. Each individual grain seems inconsequential; however collectively as time passes, the sand is spent and other uses of that time are gone forever.

It is one thing to say that poor productivity has an opportunity cost; it's another thing entirely to measure it. Like all projects, productivity related projects should be based on the same criteria that were used to justify the project's initial approval. In the case of productivity related projects, they should be measured not only on the amount of time, money, and resources they save, but also the organizational benefits gained by the use of these saved resources. The reason for this additional step is that quantifying the realized opportunity cost is the true benefit of enhanced productivity.

Now let's look at the numbers on a bigger corporate scale. Say you have $10 million total for your budget. This includes payroll, overhead, cross charges, licensing fees; basically everything. This number could be $100,000, $1 million, or $1 billion, the theory is the same, just the numbers are bigger or smaller.

What would a 4% increase in productivity mean for you? When doing your own calculations, use whatever numbers make the most sense to you given your organizational commitments, budget make up, and other related factors.

A 4% productivity gain on a $10 million budget is $400,000 in unbudgeted/allocated value. The term "value" is used versus "savings" because while some percentage of this value will be in cash, a large portion of this savings is tied up in payroll, vendor contracts, and other fixed expenses. This value relates to increased time available to your staff, additional tasks to be performed by your vendors at no extra cost, and repurposing of existing functional assets: such as software, computer hardware, equipment, and materials.

Let's analyze this $400,000 value from two perspectives: percentage of unallocated discretionary budget and revenue/profitability equivalent. Unallocated discretionary budget is the percentage of your budget over which you have full control. For example, let's say that 90% of your budget is tied up in payroll and other fixed expenses, giving you 10% left, namely $1 million for undefined business uses. This $400,000 productivity windfall represents a 40% windfall in additional business activity. Revenue/profitability equivalent is the amount of gross sales required to generate $400,000 of expense available dollars. If you have a 20% gross margin, $400,000 expense/value savings is the equivalent of $2 million ($400,000 / 20%) in increased revenue.

This book is designed to help you find these inefficiencies and convert them into opportunities; creating productivity driven success.

4. BEWARE OF THE PRODUCTIVITY MEASUREMENT FALLACY

_____

The fallacy of productivity measurement is when people try to quantify dollars saved based upon incremental productivity gains of salaried employees. Freeing up thirty minutes of a salaried employee's day doesn't save you money. By definition, the employee is going to receive the same compensation whether they are working twelve hour days or taking long lunches to sit on the beach. This time can still be of great value, just not in saved dollars because it provides time to perform additional tasks.

These thirty minutes per day have the potential to:

> _"Freeing up thirty minutes of a salaried employee's day doesn't save you money."_

» Achieve an improved work/life balance, which reduce employee attrition.

» Perform other meaningful work, which increases quality, enhances efficiency and/or shortens delivery times.

» Spend more time with their clients, which increases client satisfaction.

» Foster innovation because creative thinking requires time.

» Increase work quality since employees have more time to work on each task.

The increased productivity can show direct dollar savings and avoid falling into the "Productivity Measurement Fallacy" under the following circumstances:

» The work can be performed using one less salaried employee, who is redeployed, or removed from the organization.

» If hourly employees can perform the needed task with less over-time.

» If fees paid to consultants and/or vendors can be reduced.

» If the purchase of additional products and/or services can be avoided.

» If a task previously performed by a highly-paid employee can now be performed by a lower-paid employee and the higher-paid employee is redeployed or removed from the organization.

» If the productivity gain gives you a measurable competitive advantage against your competition, such as reduced prices, faster delivery, or other similar profitability metrics.

I don't mean to minimize the value of salaried employee productivity; to the contrary, it can be of great value. My goal here is to simply suggest that measuring your productivity efforts based on non-tangible measures can undermine the credibility of your productivity based initiatives.

Twenty years ago, I worked for a company that embarked on a company-wide productivity initiative. To their credit, they really did it right. Senior management was very involved and lead the charge. The program was clearly communicated to the employees. As incentives, prizes were given out to the teams that created the greatest company savings. All in all, it was very well done. However, the way they calculated savings was left up to each individual team to decide. Yes, we were given some guidelines, but they were very open to interpretation. So, as you may expect, since everyone wanted to win the prizes and the bragging rights for coming in first, everyone was very generous to themselves, regarding the calculated savings. In the first six months, the total savings across all teams was greater than the company's annual revenue.

The result of the poor measurement process is that the program lost credibility and was eventually cancelled; even though from a true productivity perspective, the program was a great success.

5. CLIMBING THE PRODUCTIVITY PYRAMID

_____

Productivity is never an accident. It is always the result of a commitment to excellence, intelligent planning, and focused effort.

— Paul J. Meyer

The "Productivity Pyramid" concept states that for productivity improvement activities to be effective and long lasting, they can't be randomly performed. They must be organizationally grounded, systematically implemented, and administratively supported as seen in the Productivity Hierarchy (in Figure 1). Organizationally grounded means all productivity-based initiatives must be consistent with corporate goals, holistic in nature, and consistent with organizational culture. Systematically implemented refers to the use of formalized project plans managed by the best practices, and the creation of measurable, realistic results. Administratively supported alludes to the pragmatic reinvestment of productivity savings and the tenacity to create a repeatable process that facilitates ongoing organizational improvement.

In addition to describing the steppingstones toward the creation of a successful productivity program, the "Productivity Pyramid" can also be used to assess your organization's current productivity maturity. That is to say, you can assess your organization's current ability to implement a long-lasting productivity improvement program. This can be done by comparing the Productivity Pyramid levels to your current internal capabilities. This knowledge will help you create a customized plan specifically tailored to meet your organizational needs.

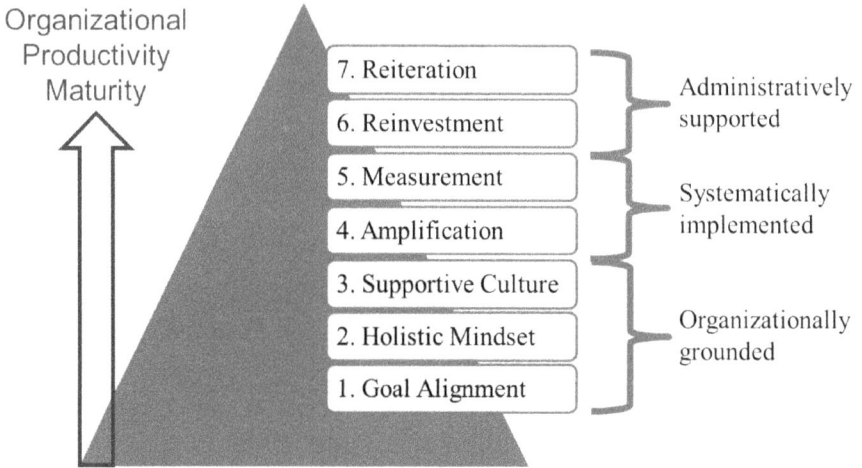

Organizational Productivity Maturity

7. Reiteration
6. Reinvestment — Administratively supported

5. Measurement
4. Amplification — Systematically implemented

3. Supportive Culture
2. Holistic Mindset
1. Goal Alignment — Organizationally grounded

(Figure 1)

Figure 1 illustrates seven key factors that are required maximize organizational productivity:

1. GOAL ALIGNMENT:

The alignment of individual, project, department, and corporate goals is a mainstay of the strategic planning process. This is also holds true for your productivity goals. As a result, as you define your productivity related activities, you must also prioritize them, based on the answers to these two questions:

> "The Productivity Pyramid is both a framework to enhanced productivity and an assessment tool of your organization's current productivity maturity."

a) Does this project free up corporate resources that can be redeployed to achieve current corporate objectives?

b) Will the project, by its nature, assist in the potential success, efficiency, or cost effectiveness of any currently funded corporate projects?

If one or more answers to the above questions are "yes", then your productivity project is a candidate for funding. Therefore like all potentially funded projects, it should be prioritized based on its short-term and long-term Return On Investment (ROI), relative benefit as compared to other projects, and other related factors.

2. HOLISTIC MINDSET:

Organizational productivity must be looked at holistically. All too often, individuals and organizations attempt to enhance their productivity through the improvement of one or two key business activities. It could be improved delegation practices, time management training, implementation of email oriented best practices or other key internal processes. Improvements in each of these areas individually have the potential to provide substantial productivity gains. However, productivity improvements in one area can cause losses in other areas. For example, an effort to reduce meetings may have the adverse effect of increasing emails. Reducing the number of people copied on emails, may cause process inefficiencies. Improved time management prioritization techniques may help facilitate individual productivity improvements, but if a team member's priorities are not properly synchronized, project deadlines can be missed and as a result, organizational infighting can counteract previous gains.

Taking a holistic view of organizational productivity can't totally counteract the adverse effects of one efficiency gain against another. However, if properly coordinated, measured, adjusted, and re-measured these effects can be minimized. For example, if you believe that reducing the number of emails will increase the number of meetings, measure the number of meetings on people's calendars prior to your email reduction initiative. Then, measure it again as the number of emails begin to decline. This is not an exact science by any means, but highlighting this potential productivity risk to those participating in the email reduction initiative effort will help reduce this unwanted side effect.

3. SUPPORTIVE CULTURE:

The role that organizational culture plays in the success or failure of your productivity initiatives were discussed at length in the Chapter 1. Remember, your productivity projects must be consistent with your organization's internal culture. If not, they will most likely fail.

4. AMPLIFICATION:

Amplification is the implementation of the various productivity amplifiers discussed in Part 2. The term amplification refers to projects that have the specific goal of enhancing (amplifying) organizational effectiveness. Like all projects, these initiatives must be defined and justified. Once selected for funding, these projects should follow the same methodologies, processes, and reporting requirements of all other funded activities.

5. MEASUREMENT:

Productivity projects should be measured based not only on the amount of time, money and resources they save, but also the organizational benefits generated. The reason for this additional step is that it defines the realized "opportunity cost" which would not have been possible without these productivity gains. It's this realized opportunity cost that is the true benefit of enhanced productivity.

All too often after a project ends, management attention is immediately diverted to the next assignment and the project is quickly forgotten. This short-term historical memory negates the possibility of an important project step. This step circles back and assesses if the benefits used to justify the project were actualized. On regular projects, such as building software or implementing a new process, the benefits are self-evident and clearly visible. However, for productivity enhancement projects, if the productivity gains are not measured, then the newfound time, money, and resources are quickly absorbed into other projects and soon forgotten. This disconnect hides the true value of your productivity related successes. In essence, if you can't count it, it doesn't count.

From a productivity perspective, there are two types of important measurement: Critical Success Factors (CSF) and Expected Productivity Gains (EPGs).

CSFs, which are a standard business practice, are the list of antidotal and quantifiable measurements that your project stakeholders will use to decide if your project has been a great success, a dismal failure, or, most likely, somewhere between. Knowing this information prior to starting the project has many advantages. First, it helps you decide if the project is doable in the eyes of those judging your professional performance. Second, it helps you define the project's scope because you know what the stakeholders are expecting at project completion. Third, it helps you be successful because you know how you will be judged at project end, so you can be sure to emphasize work in the areas where you know you will be judged.

Whereas CSFs are standard measurement for projects of all types, EPGs are specific to productivity related projects. What they do is define, in quantitative terms, the amount of time, money, and resources that will be made available for other purposes at project end. For example, if your proposed project was to enhance the speed of a process performed by ten employees, the EPG would be the amount of time and money saved from beginning to project end. If the answer is a 10% increase in productivity, the question becomes what happens to that saved 10%. If it just means that the team is a little less stressed, while that does have some intrinsic values, such as improved morale, there are no direct dollar savings. If that

10% allows the one employee to be redeployed or removed, then the EPG is the salary, benefits and overhead costs of one employee.

It's great to have defined CSFs and EPGs; however, for them to have any real business value, there has to be a specific and attainable process to collect and report the appropriate statistics.

6. PRODUCTIVITY DRIVEN REINVESTMENT:

Productivity Driven Reinvestment is an extension and application of the productivity measurement process. Simply put, it forces organizational efficiency by requiring future projects to be funded through the savings of current productivity projects.

This can be implemented in three ways. First, if you require a portion of all projects, say 10%, to be funded by productivity savings, then you drive efficiency into existing processes, while still providing needed funding for new initiatives. In effect, this forces managers to continue searching for organizational efficiencies within their existing operations and not just incrementally chase funding for the next hot project. Second, it can be used as a way to fund projects that are proposed after departmental budgets have been finalized. This gives managers a way to self-fund new department activities. Lastly, if for business purposes your organization must keep spending flat, for reasons such as declining revenues, weakening economic conditions or simply the desire to enhance profitability, then this technique can be used as a way of funding new projects, without increasing your overall budget.

Generally speaking, managers seeking project funding will not like this concept because it requires more work and forethought than simply asking for additional funds. With that said, over time, the small innovations and efficiencies it forces into the organization will provide large long term gains if properly implemented. It also has to potential to slowly modify the organization's internal culture toward a state of continual improvement.

7. REITERATIVE:

As organizations mature, one of the key factors that drive their scale and profitability is their ability to efficiently perform the same task again and again. Regarding productivity enhancement, even though each individual project may take very different forms; such as time management, email reduction, and meeting effectiveness, the overall process by which these initiatives are enacted should be as consistent as possible. The ability to drive uniformity into the productivity improvement process allows you to reap greater short term savings, as well as provide an ongoing framework that will help assure long term sustainability and maximized cost savings.

PART 2

UNLEASHING YOUR PRODUCTIVITY AMPLIFIERS

Productivity Amplifiers are business activities and concepts designed to increase process efficiency, enhance the probability of project success and help you meet your organizational goals. This is a lofty way of saying that they provide you the time, money and resources to do great things.

The eight Productivity Amplifiers divided into the following categories:

» Interactive Productivity

  › Creative delegation

  › Innovative meeting management

  › Communication efficiency

» Personal/Managerial Productivity

  › Time management

  › Leveraging the zone

» Organizational Productivity

  › Ongoing process improvement

  › Asset reuse

  › Knowledge storage and transfer

Not all these amplifiers will be right for your organization. The trick is to select the combination that best meets your current needs and helps you attain your current goals.

When deciding the technique in this section that will best meet your needs, look at it from three perspectives:

1. Which amplifiers are directly aligned with your organizational goals?

2. Which amplifiers will help be of value once your goals are attained?

3. Which amplifiers will free up the most time, money, or resources that can be redeployed toward reaching your goals.

As an example of question #1, if your goal is increased market share, then improving your sales processes or improving customer communication would be of great value. Conversely, if you are trying to increase staff productivity, then Leveraging the Zone, Time Management and Meeting Management may best meet your current needs.

Regarding question #2, if your goal is to hire a large number of engineers to replace retiring baby boomers, then Knowledge Storage and Transfer may be your highest priority. Alternatively, if building your future management bench strength is of high importance, then Constructive Delegation would be of great value.

Lastly, if your goal is to free up the maximum amount of time, money and resources to help fund other initiatives, Time and Meeting Management could slow the number of new hires and Process Improvement could reduce the costs of key processes.

If you select the wrong mix, some efficiency will be made, but you will leave potential improvements unrealized. For example, the productivity gains associated with the improvement of a manual business processes that are scheduled for replacement with automated processes has short lived value. As Peter Drucker said "There is nothing so useless as doing efficiently that which should not be done at all."

6. CREATIVE DELEGATION

Saving You Time and Helping Your Team Grow

• • • • •

Surround yourself with the best people you can find, delegate authority, and don't interfere as long as the policy you've decided upon is being carried out.

— Ronald Reagan

"Constructive Delegation" is the process of going well beyond simple task assignment but instead delegating work based on multiple criteria, including employee growth, strengths/weaknesses, cross-training, succession planning, employee retention, department throughput and other related factors. Within this chapter, your thoughts on delegation will expand beyond "who is able to do the work" to "how can I delegate in a way that enhances organizational productivity and accelerates employee growth".

I was speaking with a friend, who also teaches management training,

> *"Your thoughts on delegation will expand beyond "who is able to do the work" to "how can I delegate in a way that dramatically enhances organizational productivity and accelerates employee growth."*

about the importance of managers having the ability to properly delegate tasks to the members of their team. He told me that he was in the process of coaching a new manager who felt very uncomfortable delegating tasks to his team members because he didn't think it was right to tell others what to do. He went on to say that his client understood delegation was part of his job, but couldn't bring himself to do it.

Bob went on to say that he taught his client about:

- » Task prioritization
- » Techniques on delegating the right tasks to the right people to maximize the opportunity for success
- » The role delegation plays in team and department success
- » How to measure employee success upon task completion.

However, even with this knowledge, Bob's client still could not effectively delegate his staff. He then asked me what I could suggest that would help his client. I told him that if his client wanted to be a successful manager, he was going to have to get over it. Delegation is part of his job and if he doesn't eventually learn how, he will eventually fail as a manager.

Upon providing this suggestion, I was told that my answer seemed too harsh and insensitive. I told him that yes, it was harsh and insensitive, but also very true.

In addition to feeling uncomfortable telling others what to do, people also dislike delegation for a number of other reasons:

- » Thinking you can do it better
- » Thinking you can do it faster.
- » Thinking it will take more time to explain than to do it yourself.
- » Being control oriented and would rather do it yourself.

While all of these reasons are potentially valid, it doesn't mean managers should personally perform the task. The reason being that it is no longer their job to perform the task.

When managers continue to perform individual-contributor type tasks, the following negative circumstances can arise:

» Their team members are not given the opportunity to accomplish new and career-expanding tasks.

» They don't have time to properly perform managerial tasks because they are too focused on other tasks.

» They will most likely be viewed as not ready for managerial roles because they don't seem willing to give up their individual-contributor tasks.

Managers must also realize that doing the work is very different from managing the work. As a result, new managers must learn to gain personal satisfaction through the work of others. Of course, this is easier said than done; however, if you can make this mental leap from "doing to leading", then it will not only make you a more effective manager, but will also set you up for success.

All too often, managers head home at the end of the day feeling like they spent all day in meetings and/or watching the hard work of others. This can give them feelings of uselessness, guilt, or being nonproductive if they don't understand that their efforts are shown through the results of others. This can best be described in comparison to a symphony conductor. He/she is not playing a musical instrument, but the music would not be as beautiful without their planning and leadership.

Delegation is easy for some, difficult for many, and ultimately impossible for others. If delegation is easy for you, consider yourself fortunate. If delegation is difficult for you, it will become more accustomed with practice and experience. To those who find it impossible, you may never feel totally comfortable in a managerial role.

Given the importance of delegation as a managerial and productivity tool, the remainder of the chapter highlights specific techniques that will simultaneously help maximize your team's productivity and expand your managerial ability.

EIGHT STEP PROCESS TO MAXIMIZE DELEGATION EFFECTIVENESS

One of the great things about being a manager is that you can delegate various types of tasks to other people, versus having to do them yourself. This may sound rather cavalier, but it's true. As a manager, to do your job effectively, you must delegate various tasks to your staff. If you don't delegate, you will be overworked and your staff will be underutilized. In fact, you do a disservice to your staff if you don't delegate because it inhibits your staff's ability to learn new things and grow as professionals.

Like all management activities, delegation must be done in a thoughtful, ethical, and forward thinking manner. To that end, consider the following tips when delegating tasks to your staff, contractors, vendors and others:

1. CLEARLY DEFINE WHAT CAN AND CANNOT BE DELEGATED

As a manager, be mindful of what should and should not be delegated. For example, specific tasks may contain proprietary information that should not be shared at your staff's organizational level. Also, there are tasks that your team members may not be qualified to perform, thus setting them up for failure. Lastly, don't dump unwanted activities onto your staff to get them off your plate. Your team will eventually figure this out and it will hurt your credibility as their manager.

On the positive side, delegation can be a powerful tool to maximize your team's productivity, enhance their skill set, help them grow professionally, and free you up to perform higher level tasks. With that said, make sure that you are delegating the right tasks for the right reasons.

2. CREATE A PRIORITIZED DELEGATION PLAN

Your next step is to develop a plan outlining what tasks should be delegated to which staff member. When determining who gets which tasks, you should consider the following:

» Who is fully qualified to perform the task?

» Who could perform the task with proper instruction and mentoring with the goal of enhancing their skill set?

» Who should not be given the task because of their professional weaknesses and/or specific political situations/reasons?

» Who deserves the task based on seniority, past performance, and relevant considerations?

» The visibility and importance of the task to your department and/or company?

Delegating the right tasks to the right people is not always easy or popular; however, if you do it with transparency, fairness, and consistency, then your staff will learn to respect your decisions, even if they don't like how a specific task was delegated.

3. Provide clear instructions and define specific expectations

There is nothing worse than not been given instructions on how the task should be performed, not told what is expected, or working diligently to complete the task only to be told it isn't what they wanted. If this has ever happened to you, then you know what it is like to be on the receiving end of this demoralizing and frustrating situation. Don't be the creator of this type of situation. Give specific instructions as to what needs to be done and your expectation of the ending result. This combination of proper instructions and expectation setting not only provides the correct delegation framework, but also establishes criteria as to how he/she will be judged when the task is completed.

4. Support

When delegating tasks to your staff, particularly if this is a new experience for the employee being assigned the task, as the manager, you must be willing to provide an appropriate level of management support to help ensure success, for both the employee and the task.

The type of support provided loosely falls into two categories: mentoring and providing a safety net.

Mentoring is providing direct instruction and advice to the person performing a specific delegated task. I like to refer to this type of task-based instruction as a "learning moment" namely, just in time training on how to perform a specific task or how to deal with a specific situation. The level of instruction and/or advice to be provided should be based on the combination of the:

» Person's specific experience.

» Task difficulty.

» Political ramifications.

By a safety net, I mean creating an environment of help and protection by:

» Providing the needed resources and training.

» Allowing time to properly perform the delegated tasks.

» Helping employees navigate company politics.

» Provide instructions on how tasks should be performed.

5. LET GO AND ALLOW PEOPLE TO DO THEIR WORK

> *"If you delegate a task and then micro-manage it to the extent that you have actually performed the task yourself, it's not delegation."*

If you delegate a task and then micro-manage it, then you have not delegated properly. On the other hand, neither should you totally divest yourself from the delegated task because you are still ultimately responsible for all work performed within your department, as the manager. The trick is to walk that fine line between being overbearing and being non-participatory.

6. Give credit

As a manager, I have always believed in the philosophy of "it's the team's success, or my failure" and ask you to consider thinking this way also. This thought process causes you to raise the visibility of your staff's good work within the organization, which motivates your team members and helps instill loyalty in your staff. This approach also helps remind you that you are ultimately responsible for both your team's growth and your department's productivity and performance.

7. Actively solicit feedback from your team

Asking the members of your team if they believe you have delegated the right tasks to the right people or have provided them with the best support possible to perform the task has the following advantages:

» Reveals how you are perceived as a manager.

» Improves your team's performance by providing you with insights on better ways to delegate and support your staff.

» Shows your staff that you are willing to accept their suggestions, making you more approachable as a manager.

The Three Parts of Every Job

Everyone's job, regardless of their professional level, can be divided into three parts. Dividing it correctly enhances organizational productivity because less difficult tasks can be pushed down to lower compensated employees. Simultaneously, it also increases organizational bench strength by training staff members how to perform higher level tasks.

These parts are named:

» Must-Dos

» Hired-To-Dos

» Want-To-Dos

The Must-Dos portion of your job are those things that you get no credit for doing, but if you don't do them, then you will have problems. Generally speaking, they are thought of as the lower end of your job responsibilities. Examples of Must-Dos for a manager's role include activities such as writing employee performance reviews, formulating and tracking your annual department budget, and writing monthly status reports. All of these activities are extremely important and must be done well. In fact, if they are done poorly, there are major consequences. However, upon their completion, it is unlikely that your boss will come running down to your office and thank you for the great job you did.

The Hired-To-Dos portion of your job are those job responsibilities that you were primarily hired to perform. For example, if you are an Accounts Payable Manager, then it's your job to be sure that all of the company's bills are paid on time. Another example, if you are a Project Manager, then it's your responsibility to assure that the projects being worked on within your team are completed on time and within budget. It's this Hired-To-Dos component of your job responsibilities that will be most heavily judged from a performance perspective.

The Want-To-Dos portion of your job are those things that provide you with personal career growth by teaching new skills, providing visibility to upper management, and allowing you to demonstrate competency in new areas. As a manager, examples of Want-To-Dos may be speaking at a national conference, making a presentation to your company's senior management, covering for your boss when he/she is out of the office, or leading a cross-department company initiative.

Let's now expand this concept beyond you personally and include your staff and your manager. The low end of your job, the Must-Dos, are, in many cases, the high end of the job for those who work for you. For example, as a manager, you must review your department's budget on a monthly basis. Because this budget review is part of your responsibility you will get it done, but you know that doing so keeps you from doing your Hired-To-Dos and Want-To-Dos. However, for a member of your staff who wants to become a manager, reviewing the budget is the high end of his/her job. Now, consider the beauty of this concept and the Win-Win that it provides. If you delegate the monthly budget review to this staff member you will have the following wins:

» Win #1 - You have removed a Must-do from your plate giving you more time for your Hired-To-Dos and Want-To-Dos.

» Win #2 - You are providing career growth to a member of your staff by allowing them to review the budget. After all, for your staff member, reviewing the budget is a Want-To-Dos.

Now let's expand this concept upward from you to your boss. Comparing your manager's Have-To-Dos with your Want-To-Dos, can provide you great insight on how to move ahead professionally by volunteering to help your manger perform items that he/she view as just required tasks, but provide career growth opportunities for you. This process is also a Win-Win, but now for you and your manager.

» Win #1 - You get to perform tasks on your Want-To-Dos list that provide you with career growth.

» Win #2 - You become viewed by your manager as a self-starter and someone who is willing to take on additional responsibilities.

» Win #3 - You are freeing up some of your manager's time to work on his/her Hired-To-Dos and Want-To-Dos.

The use of this technique is not only of advantage to you, but to your manager and your staff as well; it's also an advantage to your company for the following reasons.

» It enhances company productivity and efficiency because tasks are being performed at a lower organizational level. Under the assumption that lower level also means lower compensation, the task is being performed at a lower cost to company. It also provides a more senior resource to the time to perform additional higher level tasks.

» It helps build organizational bench strength by providing on-the-job training on skills needed for employee promotion.

» It enhances employee morale, which in itself helps drive productivity and reduce attrition.

» Provides no cost employee training (except, of course, for the time spend by both manager and employee during the on-the-job training period).

PRIORITIZED DELEGATION MAXIMIZES THROUGHPUT

The concept is that if you prioritize your tasks in a way that allows you to delegate follow-up tasks more quickly, then you can create multiple streams of work that are all being done at the same time.

For example, let's say that I have three tasks to perform:

1. Write a status report for my boss.

2. Review a presentation written by a member of my staff so they can make appropriate updates.

3. Reply to a vendor answering a question related to how I want a new piece of software to be written.

The order that I personally perform these three tasks can have a dramatic effect on when all three projects are completed. If I do them in the order listed above, then neither my employee nor the vendor can begin their next task because they both need input from me before continuing. It doesn't mean that they can't be doing

> *"Prioritizing your tasks in a way that allows you to delegate follow-up tasks more quickly, creates multiple streams of work that are all being done at the same time."*

other meaningful work, it just means that they can't do the things that I need them to do. In effect, if my status report takes four hours to write, then I have delayed projects #2 and #3 by four hours each.

Because I am the "bottleneck" for #2 and #3, the obvious first step in how I should prioritize my day is to perform tasks #2 and #3 first and write my status report last. This allows both my employee and my vendor to begin their work sooner. This simple reprioritization allows me to move all three of my projects forward at the same time. In effect, I'm multi-tasking my projects through the use of others.

Now let's take one step further, which task should I do first, task #2 or task #3. The answer to this question depends on the following factors:

» The time urgency of each task

» The availability for the person (vendor or employee) to begin working on your task

» The downstream effect related to when they complete their task (i.e. is a third person waiting for them to finish before starting his/her work)

» Any financial or political advantage or disadvantage of finishing one of the tasks sooner?

» How long your work on tasks #2 and #3 take to perform?

The following mini-scenarios will help illustrate the use of these secondary factors:

First Scenario:

If your employee is waiting for your feedback (#2) on a presentation he/she is giving to a major client at 4:00 today and the vendor software (#3) is not due for completion until next month, logic would dictate that you should do the three tasks in the order #2, #3, #1.

SECOND SCENARIO:

Your employee is in meetings all morning and can't begin using your presentation feedback until after lunch; however, the vendor/software developer is sitting in the cube outside your office playing computer games (at $75/hour) waiting for your input. Logic here would dictate that you should do the three tasks in the order #3, #2, #1.

THIRD SCENARIO:

This scenario assumes that you hate doing status reports, you pro-crastinated, and now it's due in three hours. In this case, time manage-ment theory goes out the window and out of necessity you are forced to write your status report (#1) first and everyone else just needs to wait. The problem with this third scenario is that the person you are hurt-ing most is yourself because as the manager, you are responsible for the timely completion of all three projects.

The point of these three scenarios, other than to illustrate time man-agement, is to show that the use of this prioritization technique requires an understanding of how the work you do affects others and that up-front planning to reduce the need for expediting tasks that have a mini-mal effect on others.

PROGRAMMED AND LATERAL THINKING BASED DELEGATION

I'd like to begin by describing the difference between programmed thinking and lateral thinking. Programmed thinking is the process of us-ing structured methodologies or logical algorithmic processes to solve problems, make decisions, and create new product offerings. Lateral thinking is more creative than programmed thinking and facilitates pat-tern recognition, language, and out-of-the-box thinking.

Understanding this can help you effectively delegate tasks to your staff in a way that plays to each employee's personal strengths. Good managers do this through intuition and experience (lateral thinking), but by defining it, it can provide added insights and a more structured way (programmed thinking) to effectively delegate.

To see this principle in action, let's say you have two tasks you would like to delegate. The first is reviewing your monthly vs. actual budget report and the second task is writing a client proposal with the hope of gaining additional business. At first glance, you

> *"This concept can help you delegate tasks to your staff in a way that plays to each employee's personal strengths."*

may believe this is easy, namely by asking the programmed thinker to review the budget and the lateral thinker to write the new business proposal. However, this may or may not be the best move. For the first task, you may be having trouble managing your budget because business conditions and product/vendor costs have varied widely from what you had originally anticipated. Therefore, while programmed thinking is required to properly report expenditures; lateral thinking will be required to find creative ways to modify your expenses in future months to keep the budget in line. For the second task, you may think that a new business proposal would require creative (lateral) thinking to maximize the potential chance of winning the contract. Well, yes and no. Depending on the product or service you are selling, proposals may be very custom and tailored to the client or they may require following specific algorithms to be sure the client will not be under or over charged.

The key to effective delegation is twofold. First, you need to assure that the task is done well. Second, you want to delegate in a way that simultaneously sets your team members up for success and allows them to grow as professionals.

When delegating to your staff using their perceived ability as programmed or lateral thinkers as one of the criteria, take note that it should only be one of the criteria you use and that virtually everyone has the ability to do both. People may certainly lean one way or the other, but when observing people in the workplace, don't mentally box them into one type of thinking and therefore into one type of delegated tasks. I have been continually surprised over the years by the hidden and very impressive skills of those who worked for me. I have met people who I thought as just artistic, only to find they had advanced degrees in mathematics and the sciences. I have also met people who were computer programmers that I thought to be just programmed thinkers. Then, I later learned they were also great artists and linguists, with other talents that I generally associated with lateral thinking.

In closing, consider your personal strengths and weaknesses. Are you a programmed or lateral thinker? How can you use your natural thinking style to grow professionally, help your staff maximize their potential, and help your company maximize its success?

MULTI-TASKERS AND SINGLE-TASKERS BASED DELEGATION

Both multi-taskers and single-taskers are enormously important and productive and I have no preference or bias toward either work type. In fact, I find myself continually vacillating from one to the other. I have days when I find myself jumping from task to task, seemingly working on many things at once. There are also times, when I get in the zone working on a single task and can't seem to stop until that task is complete. Because I personally vacillate between multi-tasking and single-tasking; I have learned the advantages and disadvantages of each.

Multi-taskers work well in situations:

» Where there are multiple tasks and conflicting priorities as to which one should be done first.

» Where the nature of the work requires starting new tasks before finalizing other tasks.

» Where all emails and phone calls must be immediately addressed even if the current task must be interrupted to do so.

Multi-taskers underperform in situations:

» Where they must remain focused on a single task they don't like for an extended length of time.

» Many interruptions occur, but must be ignored until the task at hand is completed.

Single-taskers work well in situations:

» Where they are required to concentrate on a single task and ignore conflicting priorities and interruptions.

» Where an extended length of time is required to correctly perform the task.

Single-taskers underperform in situations:

» Where multi-tasking is required.

» Where there are a large number of interruptions that must be addressed while working on a specific task.

My suggestion to you as manager is to ascertain the preferred work styles of your staff members. Some will be multi-taskers, while others will be single-taskers, and some people, like me, can work in either mode based on the situation. Then, try to delegate tasks to each team member that plays to their personal strength and work style.

This may either be simple or nearly impossible based on the work your group performs and the makeup of your team. On the positive side, people generally know their strengths and weaknesses and will self-select jobs that best fit their personal preferences and capabilities. On the downside, your mix of required department tasks, at any given time, may not match your team's makeup. When this happens, know your switch hitters, namely those who can multi or single task and have them even out the workload.

At the risk of forming stereotypes, on average, younger workers tend to be better multi-taskers than older workers because younger workers grew up in a multi-tasking world. Older workers, of which I am including myself, grew up without email, the internet, cell phones, PCs, iPods, iPads, and even microwave ovens. In short, we had less to multi-task. As a result, multi-tasking is not as natural to me and my contemporaries as it is to my children's contemporaries. I have also read that women on average are better multi-taskers than men. That being said, I'm more of a multi-tasker by nature and my wife is primarily a single-tasker, so please take note that these are obviously generalities, not "set in stone" rules.

As odd as this may sound, it's true. As a manager, it should be just one of the many factors that you use when deciding what tasks to assign to each group member. After all, we want our team members to be successful. This is one more way you can help set up your staff members for success, not failure.

TEN DELEGATION DON'TS FOR MANAGERS

I'm often asked how to properly delegate tasks by managers taking our classes, via email from readers, in conversations after my keynote speeches, and from friends and family who think of me as the in-house "management advice guy".

The question I'm not often asked, which is equally as important as knowing how to delegate correctly, is "What things should I NOT do when delegating tasks to my staff and others?"

The reason that knowing what not to do is so important is because:

» If the task is completed poorly, you are still responsible for the project's outcome.

» Delegating a great task to one staff member may upset other members of your team who were given less interesting tasks.

» If you delegate too much to your staff, you may be seen as lazy and expendable

» Delegating the right task to the wrong person can be very demoralizing to the receiver of the task, thus reducing team productivity and potentially increase staff attrition.

» If you keep all the good tasks for yourself and only delegate the less visible and interesting tasks, then your staff may think you are selfish and not interested in their professional growth.

» Delegating tasks that your boss delegated to you personally, makes you look like you feel your boss's initiatives are unimportant.

Given the potential pitfalls that incorrect delegation can bring, consider the following mistakes and DON'T:

1. Don't delegate a task that you should truly do yourself.

2. Don't assign a task to someone who doesn't have the experience or skills to do it correctly, you are setting them up for failure.

3. Don't delegate tasks to the people you like the most. As the manager, you should be fair to your entire staff. Only picking your favorites will hurt your professional reputation and potentially reduce the project's success.

4. Don't assign a task to a staff member and then micro-manage the entire project. This is not a time saver for you and can be very upsetting to the person responsible for the task.

5. Don't assign the same types of tasks to the same people. Rotating task types among your staff cross-trains them on multiple task types, thus, widening their skill sets and increasing your managerial flexibility regarding future task assignment.

6. Don't assign a task and then not provide the needed instructions and success criteria. This lack of information will cause your staff to be unsure of how to proceed, increase stress, reduce productivity, and increase the risk of failure.

7. Don't assign a task and then not provide the needed time or re-

sources needed to complete the task. This is also setting your staff member up for failure.

8. Don't forget to monitor/measure the task's progress. Even though you delegated the task, you are still the person ultimately responsible for its success or failure.

9. Don't take credit for the work done by others. Give praise to the person who did the work. This is motivating for your team and, as their manager, you indirectly receive credit for leading a well-run and productive department.

10. Don't delegate a task that you don't really understand. Do your homework first, so you will clearly understand what you are delegating. This newly gained understanding will allow you to correctly assign the task to right person, clearly explain what should be done, and properly measure the project's progress and success.

Given all the issues previously mentioned, you may think that delegating tasks is fraught with danger and should not be done. However, delegation is a vitally important managerial skill and key factor in managerial success. The true lesson here is yes, you should delegate, but know its potential risks to help assure the success of your projects, your staff, and your professional growth.

KEY CHAPTER TAKEAWAYS

THE THREE PARTS OF EVERY JOB:

» All jobs can be divided into three parts: things you must do, things you were primarily hired to do, and those things you would like to do for professional growth.

» Knowing the three job components of your staff can help you in the delegation process.

» Knowing your manager's three job components can help you move ahead professionally.

Eight Step Process to Maximize Delegation Effectiveness:

1. Clearly define what can and cannot be delegated.
2. Create a prioritized delegation plan.
3. Provide clear instructions and define specific expectations.
4. Support
5. Let go and allow people to do their work.
6. Be mentoring and instructive.
7. Give credit
8. Actively solicit feedback from your team.

Prioritized Delegation Maximizes Throughput:

» Prioritize your tasks in a way that allows you to delegate follow-up tasks more quickly, then you can create multiple streams of work that are all being done at the same time.

» Using this prioritization technique requires an understanding of how the work you do affects others and up-front planning to reduce the need for expediting tasks that have a minimal effect on others.

Programmed and Lateral Thinking Based Delegation:

» Programmed thinking is the process of using structured methodologies and/or logical algorithmic processes to solve problems, make decisions, and/or create new product offerings.

» Lateral thinking is more creative than programmed thinking and facilitates pattern recognition, language, and out-of-the-box thinking.

» Understanding your staff's natural thinking inclinations, along with other criteria, can help you effectively delegate tasks for the good of your company and the good of your team.

MULTI-TASKERS AND SINGLE-TASKERS BASED DELEGATION:

» Ascertain the preferred work styles of your staff members and try to assign tasks to each team member that plays to their personal strength and work style.

» If the mix of required department tasks does not match your team's makeup, then use your switch hitters, namely those who can multi or single task and have them even out the workload.

» Work style should be just one of the many factors that you use when deciding what tasks to assign to each group member.

TOP THREE DELEGATION DON'TS:

» Knowing how not to delegate is equally as important as knowing how to delegate.

» Delegation is a vitally important managerial skill and key factor in managerial success.

» You should delegate, but know the potential risks to help maximize your chance of success.

7. INNOVATIVE MEETING MANAGEMENT

Maximizing Their Value and Reducing Their Frequency

• • • • •

> Staff meetings are like dentist appointments, you know they're good for you, but five minutes before the meeting, you can think of a million things you would rather be doing.

> **— Eric P. Bloom**

Your ability to run efficient and effective meetings is an illustration of your leadership ability, organizational skills, political clout, and the opportunity to dramatically move your business and professional goals forward.

This chapter discusses meetings from two perspectives: firstly, it provides insights on ways to organize and run meetings of all types. Secondly, it provides specific direction on ways to lead and enhance the quality and productivity of departmental staff meetings and other ongoing gatherings over which you preside.

THE TRUE COST OF MEETINGS

When sitting in a meeting, have you ever looked around the room at those in attendance and wondered what the cost of the meeting was to your company?

Depending on how you look at cost, this will have a major impact on your answer.

> "When sitting in a meeting, have you ever looked around the room at those in attendance and wondered what the cost of the meeting was to your company?"

From a budgetary perspective, if everyone in the room is on salary, then the people in the room are paid the same whether they attend the meeting, or not. Therefore, from strictly a dollar perspective the meeting could be considered to have no cost.

From a cost of goods sold perspective, you could say that everyone working for the company is either a direct or indirect cost of sales and/or product delivery. Using this mindset, you could calculate the hourly cost of each person in the room and multiply it by the length of the meeting in hours. Given this scenario, if the average salary of the employees in the room is $100,000, benefits and perks is 50% of base pay and overhead per employee (phone, occupancy, and etc.) is $4,000 per year, then the fully loaded cost per employee hour to the company is:

Cost of salary per hour ($100,000 / 2,000 hours per year)	$50
Cost of benefits per hour ($50 X 50%)	$25
Cost of overhead per hour ($4,000 / 2,000)	$2
Total cost per hour per person	$77
Pre-meeting setup time (5 minutes)	$6
Post-meeting setup time (5 minutes)	$6
Total cost per meeting hour	$89

Given the previous calculations, if you have ten people in your meeting for one hour the cost to the company was $890. The pre-meeting and post-meeting cost relates to the lost productivity of walking to and from the meeting. This time could be dramatically higher if the meeting is on a different floor of the building, at a different location, or if the meeting required significant post-meeting related activities, such as writing meeting minutes.

From a strict productivity perspective, 11.7 hours (using the calculation below) of employee time could have been spent performing other tasks. Please note that this amount does not include any break in concentration associated with stopping and restarting a task.

Calculation: 70 minutes per person = 60 minute meeting + 5 minutes prep + 5 minutes post

700 total minutes   = 70 minutes per person X 10 people

11.7 hours   = 700 minutes / 60 minutes per hour

Consider the "Opportunity Cost" and "Productivity Measurement Fallacy" concepts discussed in previous chapters. Unless the people in the meeting were contractors, and you could have paid them one hour less if they didn't attend the meeting, then the $890 savings is interesting food for thought, but not an actual out-of-pocket expense.

However, the 11.7 hours of Opportunity Cost is the real cost of the meeting. The natural question would be: "What else could have been done if the meeting never happened?" The answer to this question is the real cost of the meeting.

Meeting Agendas Strategies

Believe it or not, a well written agenda can enhance your meeting's productivity and help you achieve your business goals.

If done correctly, a meeting agenda can greatly enhance your meeting by:

» Setting expectations of meeting attendees.

» Keeping the meeting on track with discussed topics and subject matter.

» Helping manage the time spent on each topic.

» Allowing people to mentally prepare for the topics being discussed.

» Helping you keep away from topics you don't want to discuss in the meeting because it's not on the agenda.

» Acting as a check list to assure that all needed topics are raised during the meeting.

Also, the simple act of distributing your meeting agenda a few days prior to the meeting taking place has the following advantages:

» Allows meeting participants to properly prepare for the topics being discussed.

» Saves people who are not interested in the topics being discussed from attending the meeting.

» Helps assure that people who have a vested interest in the topics being discussed will attend your meeting.

» Provides general status information to those who cannot attend the meeting as to what you are working on.

With the advantages of using a meeting agenda now defined, the next question is "How an agenda should be written to maximize its effectiveness?"

The first and most obvious requirement is that an agenda must clearly outline the topics that will be included in the meeting and in the order they will be discussed. This may seem like a simple and straightforward task, but give careful thought as to the order that items are discussed. For example:

» If there is a topic you don't want to discuss, but are being forced to put it on the agenda, then put it last, with the goal that there might not be time to discuss it before the meeting's end.

» If there is a major issue or problem facing the group, then put it first. The reason is that if the issue is on everyone's mind, discussing it first clears the air; additionally, allows everyone to then concentrate on the other meeting topics.

» If you want to gain agreement on a controversial topic, place it near the end of the agenda, directly after three or four non-controversial items that will win easy agreement. This technique allows the group to build a momentum of agreement, thus maximizing the possibility of a settlement on the controversial topic. This approach is commonly used as a negotiation tactic.

In addition to a list of carefully ordered topics, each topic should include a start time and purpose as illustrated in the mini-agenda below:

» Meeting begins	2:00 pm	
» Topic #1	2:00 pm	For Your Information (FYI)
» Topic #2	2:10 pm	Looking for your input
» Topic #3	2:25 pm	Decision to be made
» Topic #4	2:45 pm	Update of project status
» Meeting adjourns	3:00 pm	

Including the time in the agenda helps you keep the meeting on track. For example, if there is a person at the meeting who will not stop talking about Topic #2, at 2:25 you can politely ask them to stop, so you can keep the meeting on schedule. Other advantages of including topic timing on the agenda includes; setting participant expectations as to how long a specific topic will be discussed, allowing a participant who can't attend your whole meeting enter and exit the gathering precisely when their topic is being debated and showing the importance of each topic based on its length of time in the agenda.

The topic's purpose informs invited participants why a specific item is on the agenda. This purpose has the dual effect of setting participant expectations and helping you control the meeting. From an expectation perspective, if you state that the purpose of Topic #3 is to make a decision, then people with a vested interest in Topic #3 will be more likely to attend your meeting. Regarding keeping control of your meeting, saying Topic #1 is simply an FYI, participants will not be expecting to debate the topic, and thus you can move past it quickly.

EIGHT TIPS FOR WRITING GREAT MEETING NOTES

I don't know about you, but whenever I'm in a meeting and the leader asks who would like to take the notes, I always try to find a reason to look down at my notebook as if I didn't hear him. I'm not a great notes taker and the task has never been on the top of my favorite activities. That said, there are various advantages of being the note taker and simple ways to efficiently take the notes and produce the meeting minutes.

The advantages of being the official meeting note taker and person who distributes the meeting minutes are:

» Everyone in the meeting may feel like they owe you a favor, making it easier to push through your personal agenda.

» It's less likely that you will get other, more difficult, action items because you already have to write and publish the minutes.

» The meeting will be officially documented based on your interpretation of the meeting.

» It illustrates your willingness to be a team player and take on additional tasks as needed.

» Demonstrates your writing ability.

There are a number of things you can do to simplify the note taking process, thus enhancing your personal productivity, including the following:

> "If you write the minutes, it's less likely that you will get other, more difficult, action items because you already have to write and publish the minutes."

1. Design your meeting template prior to the meeting. This helps assure that you don't miss any important items. Generally speaking, your meeting minutes should have the following categories:

   › Date, time and meeting title

   › Name of meeting leader

   › List of meeting attendees

   › For each agenda item

   » Agenda item name

   » Discussion highlights

   » Conclusions (if applicable)

   » Action items: task, person responsible, and due date (if applicable)

2. If you don't know the names of all of the people at the meeting, pass around an attendance list. This saves you from having to spend time writing down everyone's name and saves you from asking the name of someone you should know. It also guarantees that everyone's name will be spelled correctly.

3. Use bullet points whenever possible. They are easier to write and for most people they are easier to read (if they actually read the minutes).

4. Unless required, don't write down everything that was said, just highlights of the discussions, the conclusion, and the specific action items. In most meetings, almost everything else is usually worth forgetting.

5. Finalize and distribute the minutes as soon as possible after the meeting. This has the dual benefits of illustrating your professional timeliness and getting them written while the meeting is still fresh in your mind.

6. Be factual, not opinionated. Also, don't take sides in the conversation. The notes should be written from an unbiased perspective.

7. Don't try to wordsmith your notes during the meeting, it can cause you to miss an important comment that should have been recorded.

8. Lastly, if appropriate, have someone else who was at the meeting give them a quick read to be sure you didn't miss anything important or accidently report something incorrectly.

As a precaution when taking notes, be careful not to include comments or discussions that are best not documented. For example, someone speaking poorly about another employee, personal (non-meeting related) items that came up in the discussion, or arguments between meeting participants. Unnecessarily documenting these types of items could be very embarrassing for meeting participants and bring hard feelings toward you.

SEVEN WAYS OF CONTROLLING THE ROOM

As the leader and organizer of a meeting, it's your responsibility to make sure the meeting runs smoothly. As you may expect, running high quality and efficient meetings has many professional advantages including people will be willing to attend your meetings, it helps build your professional brand as a leader and assists you in reaching your meeting and business objectives.

"Controlling the room" during a meeting is conceptually similar to what professional speakers and comedians do when trying to keep the audience engaged and focused on their presentation or comedy routine. From a meeting perspective, think of the time that you had been a participant. In some of these meetings, you were fully engaged and on the edge of your seat soaking in what others were saying and trying to participate at every possible moment. Think of other meetings you attended where five minutes in you were already looking at the clock, answering emails on your smart phone, or pretending to take notes when you are actually writing out the next day's to-do list. What was the difference between these two types of meetings? In short, the answer was the leader's ability to engage those sitting in the room.

To properly engage meeting participants, you have to control the room, which requires the following:

1. To the extent possible, only invite people who either want to be there or have a vested interest in the meeting's outcome. This is easier said than done. At the minimum, try not to invite people who have no interest in your topic because they can suck the energy out of the room simply with their nonchalant body language.

2. Have a crisp, well defined agenda and stick to it in regard to both time and topic.

3. Watch the room and see who is engaged and who is fading. As you see them fade, ask them a direct question to wake them up or slightly shift the discussion (within agenda topic of course) to their area of concern.

4. Use your body language in two ways: first, to give the appearance of confidence and leadership, and second, to control the body language of others. Body language in itself is a big topic on its own. The take-a-way here is to learn more about body language if you are unfamiliar with the topic, it's fascinating and, if used correctly, can be of great professional value.

5. Start your meeting on time. If a key player is missing and needed for the first agenda item, reorder the agenda on the fly. This technique both illustrates to the participants that it is in their best interest to not be late as well as gives you the full allotted time to complete your agenda.

6. If someone is speaking on-and-on where others in the room are looking irritated and bored, then politely interrupt, thank them for the great information, and offer to continue the discussion with them "off-line" after the meeting and move to the next speaker or topic. If done correctly, you will not offend the person speaking and you will gain the gratitude of everyone else sitting around the table. If needed, use the times listed on the agenda as the reason for the interruption.

7. Don't be bored or uninterested in your own topic. As the meeting leader, your mood, body language, and energy level transfers to other attendees. The more animated and excited you are on the topic, the greater potential that your audience will be also. As a reverse example of this phenomenon, when someone in a room clears their throat or yawns, other people do it, too. This is called transference.

These seven techniques are not an exclusive list. To move forward, my suggestion to you is, that as a meeting participant, to watch other leaders run their meeting. This allows you to continually expand your leadership knowledge by observing the techniques used by others.

Seven Tips on Running Virtual Meetings

These days more and more companies are creating multi-location workgroups and allowing people to work from home, potentially jeopardizing overall team productivity. As a result, new and experienced managers alike have to learn to run meetings via speakerships, Skype sessions, and other communication tools. It may sound easy, but running an effective virtual meeting is much harder than it seems because of the following:

» People on the phone are probably multi-tasking with email or other activities.

» People in the conference room forget that people are on the phone because they can't see them.

» Meeting handouts must be emailed to remote participants prior to meeting.

» Cell phones lose service and run out of batteries.

» Location specific accents can be hard to understand.

» People joining the call late can disrupt the flow of conversation.

» Time zone differences can make it problematic to find a meeting time that is convenient for all participants.

The good news is that even with all the above difficulties, virtual meetings can be run successfully and efficiently. It just takes a little planning, a little technique, and a little practice.

Let's start with the planning. If your meeting participants are from different time zones, try to find a time that works best for all. I like to call this "the time of least aggravation". That is to say, the time that on average causes the least inconvenience to the participants. Ideally, no one should be forced to wake up in the middle of the night to join the call. Second, you must be sure that all of the documents that will be discussed on the call have been emailed to the participants in time to read and/or print them before the meeting. Finally, make sure that all participants have the conference call phone number as access code.

> *"If your meeting participants are from different time zones, try to find a time that works best for all. I like to call this the time of least aggravation for all."*

Regarding technique, there are a number of things you can do to make the call run more smoothly, including the following:

1. Place the names of those who called into the meeting on a large piece of paper next to the speakerphone. This will act as a visual reminder that people are on the phone.

2. Periodically ask specific questions to the people on the phone and require answers to assure they are paying attention.

3. If possible, if the meeting is not discussing controversial or con-fidential information, turn off the "beep" that sounds each time a new person is added to the call.

4. Connect privately with others on the meeting via Instant Messen-ger.

5. Facilitate the meeting by assuring that everyone has a chance to speak.

6. Minimize the chance of technical issues by distributing a list of do's and don'ts such as not placing the call on hold if your hold plays music.

7. Ask questions with the intent of expanding the conversation, thus not allowing prolonged silence on the call.

With the planning done and the techniques in hand, your next step is practice. If you have been a participant in a virtual meeting, but have never been the leader, it's harder to do well than it looks. If you have never participated on a virtual meeting, try to gain firsthand knowledge of how it's done by participating in one. This can be done in any of the following ways listed in order of preference.

» First, ask to join a virtual meeting being held within your compa-ny. If it is not a meeting you would normally attend, ask if you can quietly listen with the goal of understanding how a virtual meet-ing can be effectively run.

» Second, attend a free interactive webinar sponsored by a vendor in your industry. This will not only give you a sense of how virtual meetings are run, but it will also provide you the opportunity to learn something about the vendor that may help you at work.

» Third, attend a free interactive webinar on a non-work related topic, but of personal interest. This type of interactive webinar tends to be less formal and less business-like, but should give you a good idea of how a virtual meeting is run.

TEN TIPS ON RUNNING A SUCCESSFUL STAFF MEETING

Staff meetings are like dentist appointments. We know they're good for us, but about five minutes before the meeting you can think of about a thousand different things you would rather be doing.

> *"Meeting as a team helps make you feel like a team."*

However, please don't underestimate the importance of staff meetings and the very positive effect they can have on the organization's morale, cohesiveness and productivity. These effects include improved department communication, psychological team building, and improved group productivity. From a communication perspective, staff meetings enhance the communication from you to your staff, and among your staff members. Regarding team psychology, meeting as a team helps you feel like a team. Lastly, from a productivity perspective, the combination of increased communication and team cohesion helps create an environment that facilitates group collaboration, coordination, and innovation. Various tips that can help you maximize this staff meeting value are listed below. As you will see items #1 through #3 were previously mentioned.

1. Start your meetings on time regardless if some people are late, unless they are late for a known and preapproved business reason. This has three beneficial effects: first, it sends a message that people should arrive on time, it helps the meeting end on time, and provides the maximum length of time to get things done.

2. Distribute a meeting agenda at least one day prior to the meeting. This allows your staff to prepare for the meeting if needed.

3. Your meeting agenda should contain a schedule showing the amount of time spent on each topic. This has the dual advantage of keeping the meeting moving and allowing you to gracefully end discussion on topics because of time constraints.

4. Unless mission critical activities cannot be avoided, require staff member attendance. This has the dual benefit of showing meeting importance and increasing communication efficiency because all staff are in attendance.

5. Schedule your staff meetings for the same time and location each week. This consistency allows people to more easily attend and participate

6. If your meeting is in the afternoon, bring cookies or other appropriate snacks. Like Pavlov's dogs, it will help your team look forward to staff meetings because they know they will be getting a treat.

7. Schedule the meeting at a time of day that least interferes with your teams work requirements and productivity.

8. Try to make the meeting a little fun by including a short informative and fun YouTube video on an agenda related topic. This has the dual advantage of being educational for the team and also provides a little entertainment. Like providing snacks, it will help make people look forward to the meetings.

9. Always end your meetings early, or on time. If your staff meetings have a tendency to run late, it makes it hard for your team to plan the rest of their day.

10. At the end of each meeting, do a quick recap of the decisions that were made and action items that were assigned. Note that all defined action items should be assigned to a specific individual and have a specific due date. This helps ensure that the assigned action is performed.

Ten Ways to Spice Up Your Staff Meetings

Wow, there is nothing like a good weekly staff meeting to get the creative juices going and the work intensity flowing. I bet that as your reading this chapter you're thinking fondly and nostalgically about last week's meeting and you just can't wait for the next staff meeting that's coming up in just a few days. Oh boy, will it be fun, an exciting, inspirational, and altogether great time!

Oh, your staff meetings are not like this. Don't feel bad, neither are anyone else's.

We all know that staff meetings are an important vehicle for coordinating team activities, informing your staff about critical company information, and a way to build team cooperation. So if they are so important why make them a necessary evil versus a pseudo-interesting experience? The following ten ideas can help you make your staff meetings a little more tolerable and maybe a little fun.

1. Department book club

By book club, I don't mean that latest action thriller or tear jerker, I'm referring to non-fiction business-oriented books related to the work your department performs. For example, if you are the VP of Human Resources, your books could be in the area of organizational design, talent management, salary and benefits, and other related topics. If you are the VP of Information Technology, your books could be on the various IT mega-trends, such as cloud computing, big data, Bring Your Own Device (BYOD), computer security, and other related topics.

The way the book club works is that your team members are asked to read different books on a rotating schedule, having one member of your staff present a different book's key points each week. For example, if you have eight people in your department, each person would be responsible for giving a book presentation once every eight weeks.

This approach has two valuable benefits for the members of your department. First, your team is learning new key concepts related to their profession on a weekly basis. Secondly, it provides the opportunity for your staff to practice their presentation skills on an ongoing basis.

The book club also has key advantages: It provides you the opportunity to train your staff on an ongoing basis at no financial cost and has the potential to bring new concepts into your group that may be of value to implement within your department.

2. VIDEO OF THE WEEK

The video of the week is a short video, most likely from YouTube, on a business topic related to your group. It could be used as a vehicle to enhance your team's knowledge on a new technology, new government legislation, industry trend, or any other topic that you deem appropriate for your group. As an alternative to individual YouTube videos, it could be MOOC (Massive Open Online Course) shown one short video a week over an extended length of time. For example, if you are the VP of Marketing, you could use ten minutes of each weekly staff meeting to show a class segment on gamification, social media marketing, or big data analysis. Note that MOOC based classes are also free of charge.

3. CARTOON CORNER

If you are a cartoon enthusiast, then spend a fun weekend collecting copies of your favorite cartoons from your local Sunday newspaper or online source. Then, have it as an official agenda item on your staff meeting and show one cartoon each week. It's quick, it's easy, and it makes your staff meetings at least a little bit of fun.

*The only thing to consider regarding reprinting cartoons is to make sure that you have permission to do so legally.

4. VENDOR PRESENTATION

Vendor presentations are a great way to learn more about the products your team is using and/or supporting. Generally speaking, vendors appreciate the opportunity to present the new features in their latest products, better ways to work with their company via the website, or just to do a question and answer session. If the vendor is located in another city or their allotted presentation time is too short to make it worth their while to attend in person, then consider connecting them in via Skype or other online/webinar type tool. Vendor presentations are also free of charge. My one suggestion, in fairness to the vendor, is if you bring a vendor in to do a presentation, then please make sure they know it's informational and not a sales call.

5. COMPANY EXECUTIVE VISITS

Asking internal executives from other parts of your company to speak at your staff meetings has a number of great benefits. It gives your staff the chance to learn what's going on in different parts of the company and it provides a forum for your staff to meet and ask questions of senior company leaders. These questions could be about company growth, clients, policies, and other company-oriented topics. This develops a deeper understanding of the company in general, which in turn, can help your department better understand its role within the company and provide better internal service.

Another advantage of inviting senior company leaders to your staff meetings is that it gives you a reason to contact them under the best possible circumstances. In effect, you are calling them to say that you think they are very important to the company and have interesting things to say. From a political perspective, this gives you a chance to gain favor with these executives, which may be of advantage to you at a future time.

6. CLIENT/CUSTOMER STORIES

People who work in internal functions, such as Information Technology (IT), Human Resources (HR), and Finance, of large companies very often never see or hear about the company's actual clients. If you work in one of these types of functions, then it's easy to forget about what your company does and what services it provides. Asking someone from the Sales or Client Service group to speak at your staff meeting can bring real meaning as to what your company does and the role your department plays in your company. For example, if you work within IT supporting the hospital's patient records, then having a nurse tell your group a story about how an analysis feature in the software saved the life of a patient can bring a feeling of great purpose to your department's work.

7. VIRTUAL PIZZA

If you manage a virtual team, all of which are in the same time zone, say in Boston, New York, Washington DC, and Miami, have a noon-time staff meeting and order Domino's pizza for all four locations. Then, strike up a conversation on the conference call about who likes which type of the pizza the best. Not only does it bring a non-business shared experience to the group which increases team cohesion, but everyone is getting free pizza!

8. FOODS OF THE WORLD

In a second food example, say you have offices in Boston and London, have a joint staff meeting that's approximately lunch time in Boston and dinner time in London. Then serve Boston type food in London and London type food in Boston. For example, in Boston, serve fish and chips, and in London, serve New England clam chowder and lobster. This not only gives a great opportunity for discussion between the groups, but also a learning opportunity to gain knowledge on each other's culture.

9. PRODUCT PRESENTATIONS

These are presentations of your company's products and services made by a company salesperson or marketing person. The concept here is that it's valuable for everyone working within a company to understand the company's products. This knowledge can help your department better understand its role in the company, and help understand how your company's competition, as well as increase the sense of pride and loyalty that your team has toward the company in general.

10. ROTATING LEADER

The rotating leader means that a different member runs the meeting each week. The advantage of this approach is threefold. First, it adds variety to your staff meetings because someone different is leading each meeting. Second, it gives each team member experience running meetings. Lastly, it provides you, as their manager, the opportunity to observe and evaluate your staff's ability to run a meeting and lead their peers.

STAFF MEETING FORMATS

The format used to run your staff meetings can have a dramatic effect on their ability to:

» Communicate important information to your team.

» Gain an understanding of issues affecting your department's productivity.

» Build team cohesion and interpersonal communication.

» Enhance organizational effectiveness.

» Make you look like a competent manager.

Don't underestimate the power of well-run staff meetings to forward your departmental objectives and professional ambitions. Your staff meeting is the one place per week when your entire staff is able to collectively observe your leadership, organiza-

> "As a result, take your staff meetings seriously, as a place to get things done, enhance your group's capabilities, and as a venue to illustrate your leadership prowess."

tional, managerial, and interpersonal capabilities. As a result, take your staff meetings seriously, enhance your group's capabilities, and to illustrate your leadership prowess.

There are various ways to run a staff meeting. I like to classify them in four ways. When reviewing these meeting types, note that they go from less-structured to more-structured and each have their own advantages and disadvantages:

HEY, LET'S GET TOGETHER AND TALK ABOUT STUFF

This type of staff meeting is totally unstructured, has no specific agenda, and has no specifically defined topics or action plans. The advantage of this type of staff meeting is that it requires no up-front planning or forethought, your just show up and ask everyone "What's going on?" However, the downsides of this meeting type are substantial and include the following disadvantages:

- » Important topics that should be discussed are forgotten.
- » Your team has no real idea of how long the meeting will run, making it harder to plan their workday.
- » As the manager, you look unprepared. This can easily erode your team's respect and trust of your leadership.
- » Your seemingly lack of interest in your staff meeting's value and importance will cause them to follow suit and think of the meetings as unneeded and a waste of time.

ONCE-AROUND-THE-ROOM

This type of staff meeting is as it sounds. Namely, you go around the room one-by-one and everyone gets a turn to talk. During this time, they can talk about the project status, business issues, or anything else of importance that comes to mind. The meeting ends when you have gone all the way around the room and everyone has had a chance to speak.

Like the previous meeting type, this type of meeting requires no preparation, but feels much more organized and structured. Additionally, since everyone coming to the meeting knows that they will be required to speak, then they will be at least somewhat prepared, so as not to look unorganized in front of their peers and boss. Another advantage of this approach is group communication. That is to say, not only is everyone speaking, but everyone is also listening. As a result, everyone on your team gets to learn what everyone else is doing, which facilitates enhanced team coordination, group project ownership, and teamwork. However, there is a downside of this type of meeting format:

» Not everyone has something of importance to say every week. As a result, people either elaborate on unimportant items, which wastes time, or simply pass and say nothing.

» Some people don't know when to stop talking until told to stop. This can be embarrassing for the person speaking and painful for everyone who is listening and trying to be polite.

» If multiple people are working on the same project, after the first person speaks, all others working on the same project have very little to say.

When I use this meeting format, as the manager, I like to go last. That way, I can comment on what was said, bring up items of importance that were missed, and ensure the meeting ends on a positive note.

Weekly Specific Agenda

This staff meeting format is designed to be both structured and flexible because your staff has input into each week's agenda. This meeting type is best described through an example. Let's say that your group's staff meetings are on Fridays. On Wednesdays, you send an email to your staff asking them what specific items they would like to add to the agenda, whether general business issues, or other items of value. Then, you combine the following three types of topics to create that week's agenda:

1. Standard weekly topics, such as budget status, upcoming vacations, project status, and other "every week" type items.

2. Topics you would like to add to the agenda, due to company announcements, upcoming new projects, new hires, and etc.

3. The topics suggested by your staff in Wednesday's email.

There are many advantages to this staff meeting format including the following:

» It has a formalized structure, showing forethought, and also, illustrating staff meeting importance.

» It contains both standard/weekly and current topics, providing both continuity and timeliness.

» Because your staff has input into the agenda, they will be personally invested in the topic and prepared to discuss it.

» It brings issues to the forefront that, as the manager, you may not have been aware of.

As a final thought on this meeting type, putting the topics suggested by your staff last has the strategic advantage of helping you speed through the first two segments of the meeting (standard items and your topics) because your staff will want sufficient time to discuss their suggested items.

STANDARD WEEKLY AGENDA

The last of the four meeting types, Standard Weekly Agenda, has a fixed weekly format and standardized topics. In essence, it's simply the first part of the previous meeting type. The issue with this type of meeting is that it can begin to feel very stale. Additionally, as important business arises, it will need to be discussed at your meeting. As a result, this type of meeting, over time, tends to become more of an ad hoc version of the Weekly Specific Agenda format.

A second standardized format that falls under this category is the traditional meeting agenda, consisting of the following items:

- » Call to Order
- » Roll Call
- » Approval of last Meeting's minutes
- » Old Business (previously discussed items)
- » New Business
- » Adjournment

This format is generally far too formal for your run-of-the-mill staff meeting, but is ideal if you are leading an advisory committee, legal oversight, or other similar groups where attendance must be reported, formality is required, minutes must be taken and distributed, and format consistency is preferred.

CHOOSING A MEETING FORMAT FOR YOU

My first suggestion to you is don't use the "Hey, Let's Get Together and Talk About Stuff" format for the reasons previously discussed. Second, if consistent formality is required, then either of the two "Standard Weekly Agenda" types may be your best bet. That being said, for a standard general purpose staff meeting, I suggest the "Standard Weekly Agenda," because it, as stated, provides both continuity and timeliness. I further suggest that on those weeks when you don't have the time to write a formal agenda, or if you forgot to send out the email on Wednesday to solicit topics, use the "Once-Around-the-Room" format. This approach provides a little variety in your meetings and can be presented to the staff as an occasional format variation, versus being unprepared.

As a last thought on meeting format, you may find that people respond best to a specific meeting type. They may like (or dislike) a standardized format because of its predictability. They may like (or dislike) the "Once-Around-the-Room" format because it gives them the opportunity to speak in front of the whole group. So be watchful as to what is most effective, not just your personal preference as the department manager.

FACILITATION TRAINING

All this advice on agenda strategies, note taking, controlling the room, and tips and tricks may seem a little overwhelming, or at least take a long time to master. To minimize your learning curve and help maximize your ability, I strongly suggest you take a class on meeting facilitation. This is generally not offered as an internal company class because it is considered a specialty item, like public speaking. The reason it's placed in this category is because meeting facilitation if often performed by external speakers/consultants and is considered a profession, versus a general managerial skill.

The rationale behind this is the techniques you will learn are directly applicable to running great meetings and enhancing their productivity. Additionally, depending on professional role, it can be of great value when leading brainstorming sessions, group decision making, root cause analysis, and other group-related activities.

KEY CHAPTER TAKEAWAYS

> » Calculating the cost of each meeting you run will help you decide who to invite and if the meeting is worth having at all.

> » A well written agenda can enhance your meeting and help you achieve your business goals.

> » Distributing your meeting agenda a few days prior to the meeting taking place allows meeting participants to properly prepare for the topics being discussed.

> » Including the time in the agenda helps you keep the meeting on track.

> » The topic purpose has the dual effect of setting participant expectations and helping you control the meeting.

» There are many advantages of volunteering to be the meeting note/minutes taker.

» There are a number of things you can do to simplify the note taking process.

» Running high quality and efficient meetings has many professional advantages.

» "Controlling the room" during a meeting is similar to what professional speakers and comedians do when trying to keep the audience engaged and focused.

» Watch other leaders run their meeting. This will allow you to continually expand your leadership knowledge.

» Don't underestimate the importance of staff meetings and the very positive effect they can have on an organization. These effects include improved department communication, psychological team building, and improved group productivity.

» You can expand your team's knowledge about your company via company executive visits, client/customer stories, and demos of your company's products.

» You can enhance your department's cohesiveness and teamwork by providing different types of food at your staff meetings.

» Rotating the leader of your staff meeting, helps your team grow by given them experience leading a group.

8. COMMUNICATION EFFICIENCY

Better talk more action

. . . . .

> Stressing output is the key to improving productivity, while looking to increase activity can result in just the opposite.
>
> *— Paul Gauguin*

As time moves forward, there are more and more ways for employees to communicate with one another, their customers, and their vendors. As you will see, the first four communication types (one-on-one live discussion and collaboration, one-to-many communication and interaction) are based on the number of people interacting and the last two types are specific communication mechanisms. The reason for making email and social media their own categories is because of their heavy use within the workplace. While social media will primarily be discussed in the next chapter, the efficient use of email in often very fertile ground for process improvement and time savings.

These communication types fall into six categories:

» One-on-one live discussions

» One-on-one collaboration

» One-to-many communication

» Many-to-many interaction

» Email

» Social Media

> *"All forms of communication can provide business efficiencies. The issue is when any one medium is overused or not used correctly, it can become a major drag on organizational productivity and even hinder internal communication."*

From a productivity perspective, all of these forms of communication can provide business efficiencies. The issue is that when any one medium is overused or not used correctly, it can become a major deterrent on organizational productivity and even hinder internal communication. For example, the right organizational culture can reduce the hours of time spent writing long emails that will not be read, when a two minute phone call could have solved the problem. This and other similar corrective actions can harvest remarkable time saving results.

As you read about the various communication types within this chapter, consider how they can best be used within your organization. While overall productivity is organizational, communication is always personal. The trick is to create a culture, supported by the appropriate technologies that will maximize the effectiveness of interpersonal interaction, while minimizing the effort and time needed to convey thoughts and messages.

ONE-ON-ONE LIVE DISCUSSIONS

Research suggests that humans receive and interpret information from other humans in three ways:

» Words that are spoken (text or email)	7%
» Tone of voice (phone)	38%
» Body language (face-to-face or video chat)	55%

Considering the table above, while sending a text, writing an email, or picking up the phone may be more logistically desirable, they are an incomplete form of communication. This may be fine based on what is being communicated. The trick is to use the communication medium that best fits the type of information being communicated. This is based on the type and meaning of the message being conveyed. For example, logistical information, such as the time two people are meeting for lunch, can be effectively communicated on any communication medium, including text, email and phone because it's strictly factual data with no hidden meaning or risk of misinterpretation. Another example, an emotionally charged topic, such as an employee's annual performance review should be done face-to-face (or video-chat if logistically needed). This allows for the full range of human communication, particularly if the news being received by the employee is a surprise or will be viewed as unsatisfactory.

Email will be discussed at length later in this chapter. The percentages shown here, however, illustrate why emails used to communicate feelings, emotions, and/or sensitive topics are often misinterpreted, and often cause more problems than they solve.

ONE-ON-ONE COLLABORATION: REAL-TIME COLLABORATION TOOLS

Document collaboration is when two people are working on the same document at the same time. I saw this best illustrated in a TV advertisement by Google marketing their Google Docs office software suite. The ad simulated Daryl Hall and John Oates from the band Hall & Oates writing the lyrics of a song using the word processer in Google Docs.

The ad starts with Daryl Hall typing the words to the song "Man Eater", one of their most well-known songs. While typing, it shows his name above the characters being typed. When he stops typing, his name disappears from the screen, John Oates' name appeared and he began typing on the same document. It didn't show it in the ad, but if this was to be done. Then it would be ideal for the two authors to also be on the phone comparing notes and ideas.

This type of simultaneous editing can dramatically enhance document creation productivity by reducing the number of work hours needed to create the document and shorten the overall calendar time of delivery. The hours worked are reduced because it saves the participants from having to reread the document each time a revised version is passed back and forth. Therefore, the overall delivery time is shortened because the feedback loop between versions is eliminated while they're concurrently writing.

On the downside from a security perspective, many companies don't allow the use of these types of products because company documents are being stored in the cloud, outside the company firewall.

ONE-ON-ONE COLLABORATION: SCREEN SHARING

Screen sharing is also an extremely productive collaboration tool because, as they say, a picture is worth a thousand words. It's a great tool to teach people how to use new software, show someone a presentation, and perform PC technical support. It also allows for live document collaboration with the understanding that only one person can make the changes at a time, but because it is done on a shared screen, both people can see what's being done and provide immediate feedback.

ONE-ON-ONE COLLABORATION: VIDEO CHAT

Tools like Skype, that provide one-one-one video chat, have great value in the workplace. Having spoken with many companies about their virtual teams, the largest stated issue is one-on-one communication between people who have never met in person. The lack of personal interaction beyond phone and email reduces the level of understanding between people, particularly if they are from different cultural backgrounds. Video chat is not as effective as a personal meeting, but it provides great value in regard to building trust, enhancing interpersonal understanding, reducing the effect of accents and other similar advantages. Interestingly, people from long distances don't always have to use video chat to gain these benefits. Once they have been able to "put a face with the name" via an introductory video chat session, it only needs to be repeated occasionally to maintain a strong level of connection.

ONE-TO-MANY COMMUNICATION

Webinars are great communication mechanisms for presenting information to people at multiple locations. Also, because they can be recorded, they can act as both a live and an on-demand medium. Email is often used as a one-to-many communication vehicle. The danger of this approach within an office environment is that many people find the need to "reply all" to group emails. If many people feel so inclined, what started out as a simple informational comment to all can become a nuisance and clog up everyone's email with needless chatter. This issue can be solved by sending the email to yourself and Blind Carbon Coping (BCC) all other recipients. By using this approach, everyone can still email the sender, but not those who were copied on the email.

MANY-TO-MANY INTERACTION

Many-to-many interactions, whether they are in-person meetings, phone-based conference calls, video conferences, online chats, or avatar-based mediums, they all have one thing in common: they each require a skilled leader and have their own specific practices to make the meeting productive. The chapter on "Meeting Effectiveness" discusses many of these practices and provides insights into the advantages and disadvantages of each medium.

MANY-TO-MANY COLLABORATION

Many-to-many collaboration, whether in a meeting or in-person, needs structure and upfront planning to be effective. If the interaction is virtual, it also requires some simple tools you most likely already have on your computer.

To create structure, there is a brainstorming method called "Nominal Group Technique". This technique is a type of facilitated meeting where each participant speaks once and then control is passed to the next participant, similar to the concept of the "talking stick". Once everyone in the group has had a chance to speak, the cycle is repeated until all ideas/topics have been exhausted. Because there is a clear process of when people are able to talk, it works with in-person groups, fully virtual groups or a combination of both.

Regarding the process to record people's suggestions/thoughts, there are easy-to-use methods that work both in-person and virtually. The first, is simply writing a list on a white board or flip chart. If the group is virtual and video is being used, the group leader can share his/her screen and open a blank Microsoft Word document. Then, as comments are made, type them into the MS-Word document for all to see. Alternatively, rather than having the video camera pointed toward the group leader, point it toward the white board so it can be seen by the virtual participants.

Mind Mapping is a second technique that can be used record people's comments. It is a free formed diagram used to visually represent thoughts and concepts related to a single topic. It begins by drawing a small circle on the middle of whiteboard or large paper. Then, as new ideas come in, lines are drawn from the circle outward and labeled with the idea. Follow-on thoughts related to that idea are represented as branches leading off of the original idea's line. If you are working in a virtual environment and have screen-share capabilities, the leaders can share his/her screen, open Microsoft Paint and draw using the mouse. There are also various high quality software programs that can be purchased to draw these types of diagrams.

The proper use of Nominal Group Technique and Mind Mapping could each be full book chapters by themselves. If you are intrigued by the use of these techniques, there is an enormous amount of free content available on the web.

EMAIL

Email can be both a blessing and a curse. However, in all cases, it's a crucial business communication tool. The issue is that when it's overused, it can become a major deterrent on organizational productivity and even hinder internal communication. Simple practices coupled with the right organizational culture can reduce the hours of time spent writing long emails that will not be read, when a two minute phone call could have solved the problem at hand. This and other similar corrective actions can harvest remarkable time saving results for you and your staff.

When you decide to read and answer your email can have a significant effect on your personal productivity, particularly if you are a manager.

As managers, we receive emails from a number of different sources that are important to us. These sources can include:

» Co-worker based: Your boss, staff, peers, and others within your company.

» Externally based: Your clients, vendors, and etc.

» Personally based: Family and friends.

There are also a number of emails you receive which are of little or no interest to you including:

» Newsletters from vendors you don't use.

» Internal company emails you have been copied on for political, versus functional, reasons.

» Junk mail that made it through your SPAM filter.

The problem is that all these types of emails are intermingled together and have different levels of urgency. What most of us do each time our smart phone vibrates or our computer screen flashes saying mail has arrived, is to immediately look at the message and see if it's important. However, the problem is that each time you look at your email, it:

» Breaks your concentration.

» Takes time to open and read the email.

» Causes lingering thoughts related to the email that can further interrupt you from completing your current task.

» Causes restart time as you move your mental focus from your work to your email and then back again.

My suggestion to you on how to minimize the time and concentration related to reading your emails is to read them in groups, rather than one at a time. To do this, consider the following tips:

1. If deleting an email on your mobile phone also deletes it on your desktop, use normally lost time, such as standing outside someone's office waiting for them to get off the phone before you enter, to delete unwanted emails. That way, when you get back to your desk, all your unwanted emails will already be gone, thus making your desk time more efficient.

2. Turn off the automatic announcement of incoming email on both your phone and your desktop. Not to worry, when you eventually check your email at a convenient time, they will still be there.

3. Pick specific times of the day to return your emails, such as 8:00am - 9:00am in the morning, noon time, and between 4:30pm and 5:00pm before leaving the office. Doing so will not only save you from being continually interrupted throughout the day, but it will allow you to get into the "email reading/writing mental zone", which will allow you to read and write needed emails more efficiently.

4. Tell your boss, spouse/kids, and other very important people in your life that if they need you immediately, to text or call you. This will save you from being afraid that you will not respond quickly enough to an important incoming email.

5. Inform your staff and others who regularly send you emails that you respond at specified times of day. By doing so, you have set an expectation of when their emails will be returned and, over time, which many people will begin to send you emails based on when they think you will return them, thus further enhancing your productivity. For example, if I know you answer your emails at the times listed in #3 above, if I want/need to hear back from you before the end of the day, I'll send you an email just before lunch, rather than just after lunch.

6. Because you have told the people who are important to you when you answer your emails, don't create and automate email response explaining your email schedule. The reason for not using this type of auto-responder is twofold. First, the people who frequently send you emails will become annoyed by the continual auto-responses, after all, they already know your email schedule. Second, by auto-responding to spam-type emails, they know your email is live and will tell all their friends to also send you unwanted email. With this type of email, no response is best.

Like your work and/or management style, your email work style is a combination of your personality, experience, personal idiosyncrasies, and current business environment. The important take-a-way here is to assess how much of your day is spent reading and answering emails, and making meaningful adjustments.

There are a number of things you can do to maximize email's value, while simultaneously minimizing its overuse and time wasting potential:

1. Make the conscious decision that email is the correct communication medium to be used.

2. Don't write anything in an email that you don't want your spouse, kids, mother, friends, boss, customers, or the readers of the front page of the Wall Street Journal to read. Once you send an email to someone, where it goes next is totally out of your control.

3. Write as you speak. Don't try using big words, fancy language or clever turn of phrase with the hope of impressing your friends

4. Avoid using jargon, even if this is how you speak. Using phrases like "This is where the rubber meets the road" and "the 50,000 foot view is . . ." is not received well by business people who feel these phrases are overused.

5. Avoid typos at all costs. It destroys the credibility of your document. Some people won't care, but there are a large number people who immediately see typos. It almost seems that the typos just jump off the page. These gifted individuals will find reading your documents painful at best.

6. Don't tell jokes or try to be cute in your memos. It may accidently offend people.

7. Long isn't better, it's just long. Short, well-written business correspondence beats long and rambling every time.

8. Double check the spelling of people's names. Debbie is sometimes spelled Debby and John is sometimes spelled Jon.

9. Be careful when referring to people you don't know. Chris, Terry, Jo, and other names that could be unisex. Also, double check the gender and spelling of people from countries and ethnic backgrounds of which you are not familiar. It can save you from an embarrassing mistake.

> "Don't write anything in an email that you don't want your spouse, kids, mother, friends, boss, customers, or the readers of the front page of the Wall Street Journal to read. Once you send it, where it goes next is totally out of your control."

10. Save all of your emails and written documents for future use. Business issues and situations tend to resurface. Having your old correspondence within reach can save you the time of rewriting it from scratch.

11. Know your audience. If the key person/people receiving the email like bullet points, then write bullet points. If they prefer detailed written text, then write detailed written text.

12. When writing an email to a specific person or persons, remember to use good manners. That's please, thank you, and other appropriate pleasantries.

13. If you are unsure if your email properly reflects the business issues, ask someone you trust/respect to read and critique it first before you send it out. Emails should always be written in a way that it could be read by everyone without offence. Always remember that a single email written in an inappropriate way can cost you your job.

Remember that your written word represents your abilities and professionalism. Consider this every time you press the "Send" button. Also know that once published, it will be difficult, or impossible to retrieve.

SOCIAL MEDIA

As you will see in the next chapter, social media, if used correctly, can be a very effective employee communication tool as well as a way to collect, retain, and distribute corporate knowledge.

KEY CHAPTER TAKEAWAYS

» If any one medium is overused or not used correctly, it can become a major deterrent on organizational productivity and even hinder internal communication.

» Use the communication medium that best fits the type of information being communicated based on the type and meaning of the message being conveyed.

» Assess how much of your day is spent reading/answering emails and making meaningful adjustments as needing.

9. TIME MANAGEMENT

_____

Spending Time Like it's Money

● ● ● ● ●

There is never enough time to do everything, but there is always enough time to do the most important thing.

— Brian Tracy

When I think of time management, I like to think beyond the typical cast of characters, such as to-do list, ABCD, President Eisenhower's Principle (Important and Urgent, Important and Not Urgent, Not Important But Urgent, Not Important Not Urgent) and other commonly used techniques. These techniques are great and truth be told, I live off of my to-do list and often use Eisenhower's Urgent/Important Principle as a way to filter out unimportant tasks. However, when it comes to time management, these types of tools are the required baseline, not the pinnacle of efficiency.

The techniques described in this chapter aren't your typical time management practices. You can learn those anywhere. These techniques are a combination of concepts that, if internalized and used properly, can help maximize you and your department's productivity.

PROTECT YOUR SCHEDULE USING THE "NEAR-TIME FAR-TIME" CONCEPT

As an executive, very often the most limited resource is your own time. This concept has three great benefits:

> "The techniques described in this chapter aren't your typical time management best practices. You can learn those anywhere."

1. Helps protect you from filling your schedule with meetings and events that are less than optimal toward meeting your business goals

2. Used in reverse, helps you schedule time with other busy people

3. Used in reverse, helps you secure the best possible people for your future projects

This may seem like extraordinary advantages for a time management technique, but it's true and this is how it works.

The underlying principle behind this technique is that people are much more protective of their commitments and schedule in the near-time (the next two or three weeks), rather than scheduling their far-time (the two or three months from now). The reason being that people generally have a strong mental picture of their short term:

» Business commitments and work deliverables.

» Longer range projects nearing their delivery dates.

» Problems which have arisen and must be dealt with.

» Unforeseen business opportunities that have seemingly come out of the blue.

» Personal time commitments, such as doctor appointments and kids' soccer games.

» Uncomfortable feeling that your calendar is so filled with meetings that you will not have time to complete/perform the previously mentioned items.

For all of these reasons, busy people are very protective of their short-term time because they can mentally calculate their workload.

People's far-time schedule is much less defined:

» Many business commitments and work deliverables have not yet been assigned.

» Long range projects are still viewed as being long-range.

» Future problems have not as of yet reared their ugly heads.

» Unforeseen business opportunities are still unforeseen.

» Doctor appointments have not yet been scheduled.

» Children's future soccer schedules have not yet been emailed to their parents.

As a result of these future unknowns, peoples' future calendars and time commitments always seem to be less overwhelming and thus, they are more willing to add meetings to their schedules and commit to personal deliverables.

The suggestion here is to be as protective of your far-time as you are of your near-time. The reason is that time marches forward. Two or three months from now, today's far-time, will become tomorrow's near-time. The further in the future that you try

> *"Be as protective of your far-time as you are of your near-time. Two or three months from now, today's far-time, will become tomorrow's near-time."*

to schedule a meeting, the more likely it is that your meeting request will be accepted. Of course, there is the potential that the person will reschedule or cancel the meeting as time gets closer. However, if they do, then they will be less likely to cancel a second meeting. In addition, when trying to schedule future meetings, be careful not to request days during known busy times for the person you are targeting. For example, if you would like to meet with the VP of Sales, don't try to schedule the meeting the last week of the month, quarter, or year. They will most likely want to leave these times open to close pending deals within the current period. Requesting a meeting at these times shows a lack of understanding of their workflow.

Managers are generally more knowledgeable at securing the best future project resources of their current resource requirements than their future resource needs because current projects have not yet run late, future requests have not yet been asked, and future production and business issues have not yet come to light.

Physical exercise can help improve your team's productivity

Did you know that certain types of exercise counteract the effects of poor posture endemic to people who work at desk jobs? Or that there are stretches you can do at your desk that can help improve your health? Did you know that exercise helps delay cognitive decline and can help maximize the productivity of middle age and older workers? Well, I didn't either until I spoke with Ellen Cohen-Kaplan, an occupational therapist and personal trainer.

It's been well documented that an appropriate level of regular exercise aids overall health and life expectancy. What I didn't know was that this same exercise can also help your productivity at work. Encouraging and helping to facilitate athletic activities of your staff is not only good for them personally, but it can also make them more productive in the workplace. For example, research has shown that exercise helps increase your mental processes, memory, and so-called executive functions. These functions include planning, organization, and the ability to mentally juggle different intellectual tasks at the same time.

Ms. Cohen-Kaplan went on to say that there are exercises you can do in just a few minutes while sitting at your office desk, or standing next to it. For the exercises listed below, start at your neck and work their way down your body. Beforehand, consult your physician to assure you are of appropriate health to perform these exercises:

» Rotate your head from left to right and then up and down - these movements help stretch and relax your neck muscles.

» Raise and lower your shoulders, then move your shoulders forward and backward. Emphasize and stay in the "shoulders back" position for a count of 5. This loosens your shoulder muscles and helps reduce stress.

» Hold your hands behind your head and push your elbows back. This back extension helps further stretch your shoulders as well as your upper back.

» Place your left hand on your right hip while rotating your spine to the right and trying to look over your right shoulder. Then, perform the same move to the left side. These back rotations help stretch and relax your lower back muscles.

» Stand up, bend forward, bend your knees and put your hands flat on floor. Then, try to straighten your legs while keeping your hands on the floor. This stretch helps loosen your hamstrings which can become tight from sitting for prolonged periods.

» Perform leg lunges by putting one foot forward, bending your forward leg while keeping your back leg straight, and having your back heel up and your back toes on the floor. This position will help stretch your thigh muscles and loosen your lower body.

Some interesting points related to your workplace include:

» Sitting with hunched posture and leaning forward toward your desk can cause shallow breathing which causes your body to receive less oxygen, which can lead to fatigue and lower cognitive functioning.

» Ergonomically, placing your computer monitor at eye level, so your neck is neither flexed forward or back, is the best way to design your workplace.

» Sitting for more than half an hour without standing for a few minutes to stretch can tighten your muscles and reduce your productivity.

In the long run, helping to facilitate your staff's health has true business benefits, including reduced absenteeism due to lower occurrences of illness, helping prevent chronic diseases like diabetes and heart disease helps decrease heath care costs, and being seen as a boss interested in your team's health can help you attract and retain top employees.

Encouraging your staff to exercise and exercising yourself is not only good for you and your team personally, but it's also good business. It's a true win when your employees' goals and well-being directly align with business objectives. Physical exercise is a prime example of employee/employer alignment. It's also another form of bonding.

> *"Encouraging your staff to exercise and exercising yourself is not only good for you and your team personally, it's also good business."*

SPEND TIME "ON" AND "IN" YOUR DEPARTMENT

The idea of spending time "on" and "in" your department is best described using the example of a small person consulting firm specializing in management consulting. Like most small companies, the owner, has two primary responsibilities; first, generating revenue by doing hands-on consulting and second, trying to find future consulting assignments. The problem is that if you try to maximize your revenue by spending all your time working on your current client, then when your consulting engagement ends, you don't have your next client lined up. Alternatively, if you spend too much time marketing, you run the danger of not properly servicing your current client or reducing your billability.

Department managers have a similar dilemma. That is to say, if you spend too much time "in" your department working on tasks performed within the department, you don't have time to properly manage your staff or perform manager-level tasks such as salary planning and budgeting. Alternatively, if you spend too much time "on" your department, performing general management functions, then you run the risk of not properly managing your staff.

One of the hardest things for self-employed consultants and new managers is to properly divide their time between these two types of activities. This phenomenon is doubly true if the manager is in a player/coach type role where he/she officially has both managerial and individual contributor type responsibilities. Some of the reasons that this balance is hard to achieve are:

» The pressure to complete department tasks on time and under budget prevents you from performing required administrative processes.

» It's more fun and personally gratifying to perform the tasks you like best (management or task oriented) and ignore other important tasks.

» It takes great discipline to go outside your comfort zone and work on items that you know should be done, but are afraid you can't do properly and/or are intimidated with the task in general.

» If you are a procrastinator by nature, it can be easy to delay work on managerial processes, such as writing performance reviews, particularly, if you have more interesting tasks to keep you busy. Then, you wake up one morning and realize that it's virtually impossible to get them all written in time to meet the required deadline.

Even under the best of circumstances, properly dividing your time between responsibilities can be extremely difficult, as anyone knows who has ever been in a professional role where you were 50% allocated to one task and 50% allocated to another. Unless you are very good (or very lucky) one of the tasks takes a back seat to the other or you find that you end up having two jobs, seemingly 100% allocated to each.

All that said, as a first-line manager or to anyone who has both supervisory and individual contributor type responsibilities, the following time management tips can help you manage your day:

1. General manager-related activities, such as writing performance reviews and budgeting, are generally scheduled months in advance. Put them on your calendar as soon as possible, even if they are months away.

2. Place meetings on your schedule just for you. These "me-only" meetings have two advantages. First, they build time into your day to get your important, but not immediately required tasks done in a reasonable timeframe. Second, if an important issue arises, you will have a little flexibility in your schedule by converting your "me-only" meetings to other activities.

3. Delegate, delegate, delegate. One great things about being a manager is that part of your job is to tell other people to do things. If you are overwhelmed with the quantity of work, hand off some of it to the people in your team. Always remember: just because you have delegated the task, you are still ultimately responsible for its completion. So after you delegate, delegate, and delegate, remember to follow up, follow up, and follow up!

4. Prioritize your work and the work done by your department. As the expression goes, you can only fit one gallon of milk in a one gallon bottle. No matter how hard you work or how hard you push your team, there is only so much time and effort that can be expended. Proper prioritization will allow you to get the most important items completed and still hopefully provide a reasonable work/life balance for you and your team.

5. Work smart, not just hard. Look for tasks performed by you and

your department that could be done more efficiently, or potentially not at all. Removing tasks from your plate provides you with more time to do other things. Removing and/or streamlining tasks performed by your team lightens their work load, providing you with additional opportunities to delegate your work to your team.

In closing, properly managing your time is not a panacea that will miraculously give you all the time you need to properly perform all your "on-department" and "in-department" tasks, but it can surely help.

PLANNED MULTI-TASKING ENHANCES THROUGHPUT

As a manager, it often seems that you are required do many things at once just to survive, let alone succeed. If this is you, there are a number of easy multi-tasking techniques you can use to help you maximize your productivity:

1. Delegate parts of tasks: One of the great things about being a manager is that you have the authority to delegate tasks to those who work for you. If used correctly, delegation can be used to let your staff help you multitask. For example, if you are trying to select a vendor to perform a specific task for your department and this selection process requires analysis of each company's products, write a short questionnaire and three members of your team each to analyze one company. This process will not only personally save you time, but it will also get the overall job done very quickly.

2. Pair up complimentary tasks: There are some tasks that require intense concentration and some that require an occasional bit of attention. For example, say you have two tasks to complete today, one is creating a presentation to give to a major client, and second, print a number of different spreadsheets that have to be printed one at a time. These two tasks are wonderfully complementary because each time you need a mental break from writing your

presentation, you can mindlessly print another spreadsheet. Also, if you get deeply into the zone on your presentations, then there is nothing related to the spreadsheet task that would inconveniently break your concentration.

3. Answer emails in bulk, not as they come in: Answering emails in a group, rather than one at a time, reduces the mental time and energy needed to switch between tasks. For example, if you answer an incoming email every ten minutes, then you will not have more than ten minutes of uninterrupted time on any other task. It may seem counterintuitive to batch your email for those that pride themselves on responding quickly to those they serve; however, your willingness to answer emails first thing in the morning, just after lunch, and at the end of the day could help enhance your productivity to the point that it may make it easier for you to meet your deadlines; therefore, enhance the quality of your deliverables, and maybe even write more insightful emails because you will be answering them more efficiently.

4. Recover from one activity by doing another: This is actually a technique I first learned when trying to speed up my weightlifting training in the gym. As an example, the way that I would rest my biceps between sets of dumbbell curls would be by doing a triceps exercise that worked the opposing muscle group (the muscle on the back of my arm). This allowed me to get twice as much exercise in during the same lunch hour. This technique can be used within the workplace by picking two tasks to work on that allow you to rest one mental or physical faculty by doing the other. As an example, I have a training company named Manager Mechanics. We teach IT professionals to be managers. As a result, I spend a fair amount of time developing new or customized training materials. This task requires the creation of textual materials and graphics. When I get tired of the left-brain activity of writing text, I change my activity to the right-brain task of selecting the graphics that

will be used to accompany the textual materials. The switching between writing and graphics selection helps keep me fresh on both activities.

These four techniques work for me and I hope they can be of value to you also. As a last recommendation, don't stop with these four techniques; try to discover others that work for you. The more techniques you find, the more efficiently you can work; which results in a greater chance you will meet your work deadlines, enhance your work quality, and even potentially enhance your professional success.

REQUIRED WORK VS. REQUESTED WORK

If you are the manager of a company department that is providing services to people in other internal departments, your work can generally be categorized in two ways: Required Work and Requested Work.

Required work can best be described as the ongoing processes that your department performs day-in and day-out. It is basically your department's core function and purpose. Examples include: running the company payroll, producing budget vs. actual reports, or working on the Technology Help Desk and assisting employees with their computer-related problems.

Requested work are tasks that are related to the work your department performs, but are not your department's primary function. They are directly requested by fellow employees in support of a specific project being performed. Note that I am by no means saying that these work requests are not important; they may be in support of a major company initiative, or needed research to correct an overwhelming company problem.

To further explain the difference between required and requested work, consider the job of the electric company. Their primary job is to make sure that your home or office has a continual flow of incoming power 24 hours a day, 7 days a week. Note that many locations around the country and around the world, the electric company also performs a secondary task of helping their customers reduce their power needs by performing energy audits and giving out more efficient (lower energy) light bulbs.

My question to you is this: "If the electric company only had time to perform one of these two tasks (keep your power on or perform a requested energy audit), which task would you rather they do?" My guess is that you would rather they keep the power on. This is the difference between required work and requested work.

Let me take this one step further. Have you ever heard your alarm clock go off in the morning right on time and then immediately call the electric company to thank them for keeping the power on all night so you could get to work on time? I think not. What happens is that, over time, we expect the power to always be on and as a result; therefore, we take it for granted and get very upset and feel very inconvenienced when it's not working.

The moral of this story is that if you do it well, the core functions that your department performs will be taken for granted by your fellow employees. With that said, they may never call to say thank you, but you will definitely hear from them when a problem occurs. Reading this concept may make you upset, thinking that your department's great production work is being taken for granted by your co-workers. If you are feeling this way, then think of this: when was the last time you called the payroll department to thank them for once again correctly depositing your paycheck into your bank account? Most likely, never.

My advice to you is to never allow your required work to suffer by too highly prioritizing incoming requested work. Certainly do your best to

> *"When was the last time you called the payroll department to thank them for once again correctly depositing your paycheck into your bank account? Most likely never."*

help all those coming to your office door in need of favors or special requests; just don't give them so much attention as to put your core production processes in peril of failure. If you do, you will quickly find that the criticism you receive related to failing at your primary mission will far outweigh the praise you will get by helping one person on a special project.

TEN PLACES TO FIND DEPARTMENT PRODUCTIVITY KILLERS

My manager once told me that his department was very overworked, which resulted in his team being burned out and wanting to quit. He went on to say that he could not reduce his department's workload or hire additional people. He asked if I could give him any suggestions on how he could deal with this issue.

I agreed that he was in a difficult situation and I give him credit for trying to find ways to give his staff some relief. Given that he couldn't reduce his department's workload or increase his staff, my advice to him was to look for:

1. Processes that can be streamlined.
2. Non-mission critical tasks that can be postponed or discontinued.
3. Internal department projects that can be postponed.
4. Reporting processes that can be redesigned.

What the above items have in common is that they reduce team activity. Having a keen eye for these productivity killers can have the effect of reducing a team's workload through the combination of fewer or improved processes and the removal of unrequired tasks.

A second potential way to reduce a department's overall workload is to look for things outside the department that have an adverse effect on the team's productivity. These types of items include:

1. Calls coming in from outside the department that reduce team performance.

2. Cross-department projects in which your team members have been asked to participate.

3. Required corporate training classes that can be temporarily post-poned.

4. Work coming to your group in the wrong or incomplete format, thus requiring extra work/processing/time by your department.

Lastly, look for modifications to the input and output of department deliverables that could enhance overall productivity. These types of modifications include the way information is sent to your department, with the goal of reducing the preparation time needed to prepare incoming work for processing and ways to modify your department's product output in a way that still meets your clients' needs, but is easier for your team to produce.

The trick here is to carefully analyze your department's tasks, processes, obligations, and distractions in search of opportunities for incremental productivity improvement. Over time, multiple small improvements can have a very positive effect on your team's overall productivity and morale. Productivity improves for three primary reasons: there is less work to do, the tasks being performed each take a little less time, and there are fewer interruptions. From a morale perspective, your team will certainly enjoy having a little less work, but they will also truly appreciate that you, as their manager, are doing everything you can to reduce their workload.

As an additional suggestion, analyze which tasks are assigned to each employee. Some people can do things faster than others; therefore, find the opportunity to modify staff assignments with the goal of assigning tasks to the person that can complete them the most quickly and efficiently.

Also, don't forget to analyze your own workload, processes, and responsibilities. Upon this analysis, you may find some small ways to improve your own productivity. This will give you more time to optimize your team's productivity and even take on a task or two yourself.

TEN THINGS YOUR DEPARTMENT CAN DO DURING SLOWER WORK TIMES

Many jobs have work cycles. Accountants tend to be busiest at the beginning of each month, when trying to close the books from the previous month. Sales people tend to be busiest just before month end trying to close deals before the period ends. Other jobs also have daily, weekly, monthly, and/or yearly busier times and slower times.

There are things you can do to help your team renew their energy, maximize their productivity, and maintain their motivation during the less crazy times in their natural business cycles:

1. Celebrate the end of each difficult/hectic business cycle with a department lunch. If you don't have the funds, then make it a "pot-luck" lunch where everyone brings a different type of food to share. If you don't think a pot-luck will go over with your group, you can just have everyone bring their own lunch.

2. Have a speaker come to an extended staff meeting, teaching your team something new. It could be an internal company executive from another part of the company, a vendor, or even a senior member in your team.

3. Show videos at an extended staff meeting. This is easy and free. Do a little research on YouTube and find instructional and entertaining videos that relate to your team's profession and activities.

4. Have a "Floating Friday Afternoon", allowing one or more of your staff to leave work early, based on some pre-organized and fair scheduled basis.

There are also things you can do to help maximize your team's productivity:

1. Have a brainstorming session analyzing how existing internal department processes can be streamlined.

2. Have a brainstorming session analyzing what new processes should be created.

3. Have a "Clean your office day". This may sound a little odd as a productivity tool, but generally speaking, people can be more productive if your personal workspace and department workspace are clean and orderly.

Lastly, there are activities that will help maintain staff motivation:

1. Cross-train members of your team on each other's jobs. This provides free training to your team and increases your future job assignments as their manager.

2. Have mini one-on-ones with your team members with the goal of helping them to grow professionally.

3. Have your boss come to a staff meeting and answer company-related questions for your team.

If your team is working full throttle on an ongoing basis, the thought of downtime to do any of the above activities may seem unrealistic. For your team, the above activities can help save your team members from burning out, or at least not burning out as quickly. That being said, try to do abbreviated versions of the above activities. Instead of doing an extended staff meeting with a speaker, have a speaker for 15 minutes during a staff meeting. Call an impromptu staff meeting on a Thursday afternoon from 4:30 to 5:00 and instead of talking about business, show a short five minute business oriented video on YouTube, thank your team for doing great work and working so hard, and send them home twenty minutes early.

These types of activities, big and small, can help make work a little more fun and interesting. This in turn will help you energize your team, thus maximizing their productivity, motivation, and overall morale.

> "If your team is working full throttle on an ongoing basis, the thought of downtime may seem unrealistic. For your team, these activities can help save your team members from burning out, or at least not burning out as quickly.

KEY CHAPTER TAKEAWAYS

PROTECT YOUR SCHEDULE USING "NEAR-TIME FAR-TIME"

» People are much more protective of their commitments and schedule in the near-time (the next two or three weeks), versus they are of their far-time (out two or three months from now).

» Be as protective of your far-time as you are of your near-time.

» Use this technique in reverse when trying to schedule meetings and/or gain commitments from others.

EXERCISE CAN HELP IMPROVE YOUR PRODUCTIVITY

» It's been well-documented that an appropriate level of regular exercise aids overall health and life expectancy.

» There are exercises you can do in just a few minutes sitting at your office desk or standing right next to it.

» Encouraging your staff to exercise and exercising yourself is not only good for you and your team personally, it's also good business.

SPENDING TIME "ON" AND "IN" YOUR DEPARTMENT

» If you spend too much time "in" your department working on tasks performed within the department, you don't have time to properly manage your staff.

» If you spend too much time "on" your department, performing general management functions, then you run the risk of not properly managing your staff.

» The combination of time-saving techniques, proper time prioritization, and self-discipline can help you strike the proper balance between working "in" and "on" your department.

PLANNED MULTI-TASKING ENHANCES THROUGHPUT

» There are a number of easy multi-tasking techniques you can use to help you maximize your productivity.

» Effective multi-tasking will help you meet your work deadlines, enhance your work quality, and even potentially enhance your professional success.

REQUIRED WORK vs. REQUESTED WORK

» Required work can best be described as the ongoing processes that your department performs day-in and day-out.

» Requested work are tasks that are related to the work your department performs; however, they are not your department's core primary function, and are often directly requested by a fellow employee.

» Never allow your required work to suffer by too highly prioritizing incoming requested work. The criticism you will receive related to failing at your primary mission will far outweigh the praise you will get by helping one person on a special project.

TEN PLACES TO FIND DEPARTMENT PRODUCTIVITY KILLERS

» If your team is overworked and there is no relief in sight, look for ways to streamline your processes, postpone, or discontinue non-mission critical tasks, which will reduce interruptions that come from outside your department.

» Additionally, analyze your own workload with the goal of freeing up time to help your team on needed mission critical activities.

TEN THINGS YOUR DEPARTMENT CAN DO DURING SLOW TIMES

» Many jobs have work cycles.

» There are things you can do to help your team renew their energy, maximize their productivity, and maintain their motivation during the less crazy times in their natural business cycles.

10. LEVERAGING THE ZONE

Magnifying your creativity and output

· · · · ·

Productivity is being able to do things that you were never able to do before.

— *Franz Kafka*

Let me begin by explaining my concept of being in the zone. Being in the zone is when you are:

1. Mentally clear on the task to be performed.
2. Highly focused on a specific task.
3. Physically able to perform the task.
4. Motivated to perform the task.

By Mentally Clear, I mean having an exact understanding of what you want to do. It could be something simple, like deleting spam email, or something intense, like designing the new structure for your company's communication backbone. This lack of ambiguity and an understanding of the task at hand allows you to move forward without a feeling of doubt, ambiguity or need for further direction.

By Highly Focused, I mean single-mindedness, namely, being able to free yourself from mental distractions, like thinking about other projects, all the emails you must answer, or a presentation you are making later in the day. This single-minded purpose helps keep you concentrate the task at hand.

By Physically Able, I mean that at this moment you are able to perform the task. For example, I know that if I'm very tired, I have great difficulty doing mentally challenging work like writing documents, answering important emails in a concise manor, or making important decisions. This provides you the energy to begin the task and the endurance to complete it.

By Motivated, I mean is this a task that you want to (or have to) work on right now, providing the proper incentive to begin working on the task.

MAXIMIZE YOUR PRODUCTIVITY USING ZONE LEVEL PRIORITIZATION

I know anecdotally by speaking with others, that when people are truly in the zone on a task, regardless of the task's simplicity or complexity, you are more productive, more innovative, and more likely to do a better job. This powerful combination of productivity, innovation, and quality is why we should strive to be in the zone on any task we are performing.

Your Highest Zone is the task at that time that best fits the above descriptions. Using a previous example, if I'm mentally exhausted and have two hundred emails to review, my highest zone work at that time may be simply deleting spam and other irrelevant emails from my inbox. Alternatively, if I am mentally alert, the deadline for my next column is quickly approaching, and I have a great topic idea in mind, I'll write my column, regardless if my email inbox is a mess.

Given these two examples, it would be a mistake for me to spend my time deleting emails, if I have the ability, motivation, and focus, to write my column. I can delete my old emails later, when I am less mentally sharp. The final lesson for you here is mentally dividing the items on your to-do list by zone levels. These levels could be named:

1. When I'm at my best.
2. Business tasks I can do on auto-pilot.
3. Busy tasks that must be done, but don't require mental challenge.
4. Things you do as long as you are not asleep.

Then, pick the task to be performed based on your physical, mental, and motivation at that time.

In addition to using this technique to enhance your personal productivity, as the department manager, you can also enhance your department's productivity by doing the following:

» Teach this concept to your staff to help them maximize their productivity.

» Always assign tasks to each staff member related to all four levels; therefore, allowing them the flexibility to implement this time management strategy.

» When possible, provide appropriate lead time on deliverables to not force high level work during low level zone efficiency.

» Understanding the general times of day when your team members are not in their highest zones; therefore, allowing you to schedule meetings and other low-energy activities at appropriate times.

If used correctly, this concept alone can dramatically enhance your personal productivity, the productivity of those on your team, and as a result, your department's overall performance and efficiency.

MANAGEMENT TIME VS. WORKER TIME

As managers, we work in 30 minute and 60 minute time frames. That is to say, our schedules tend to be filled with half-hour and one-hour meetings. We learn how to efficiently move from topic to topic, conference room to conference room, and committee to committee. Our hands on work, such as answering emails, writing performance reviews, writing status reports are also done in 30 and 60 minute timeframes because we work on them in between meetings. I'm not making a value judgment as to whether this is good or bad, I'm simply making a statement that this is how it is. For a busy manager to survive, they must learn to work under these circumstances. Unfortunately, the more senior your job becomes, the harder it becomes.

Knowledge workers, who are employees that are hired to work more with their minds than their hands (such as computer programmers, writer, analysts, etc.), tend to work in three hour segments. That is to say, they start working on a particular project: for instance, writing a computer program, designing a building, developing a marketing plan, etc. They get into the zone. They are totally engrossed with the task and a combination of insights, creativity, and high productivity are the result.

> *"Knowledge workers tend to work in three hour segments."*

Speaking for myself, as a knowledge worker, when writing books, designing and developing new management training classes, or when writing a new keynote speech; I get in the zone and could go on for hours, until I get hungry, fall asleep from exhaustion, or nature calls.

The problem is when you try to impose your schedule onto a knowledge worker's day. If you do, you destroy their creativity and productivity. Not to mention, destroy their morale and motivation. To avoid this please consider doing the following:

» Plan your staff meetings around natural breaks, most notably, first thing in the morning, just after lunch, or at the end of the day.

» If they look deep in thought, don't interrupt them, once out of the zone it's difficult, or basically impossible to get back to exactly the same place.

- » If appropriate, given the option to go to a meeting, versus requiring it.

- » Have meetings at predicable times, so they can plan their work around them

- » If they are in cubicles, let them wear headphones as long as they can hear the fire alarms and are not bothering other people.

- » If possible, don't have your best knowledge workers in cube on main walkways, loud employees and hallway conversations can break their concentration.

As a manager, this may sound like you must really go out of your way to make those in your group more productive. Well, yes it is because you should! After all, the more productive they are, the better it is for the company; therefore by association, the better it is for you.

When I was in a management role, it was never below me to do the coffee run or do the photocopying if that's what it took to get the job done. I believe that as managers, it's our job to make our team as productive as possible. Back to the topic at hand, if that means trying to schedule meetings around my team's "zone time", then I'll try to do it and suggest that you consider doing the same. I know that when I was a knowledge worker doing software development, business analysis, software testing, or other similar tasks, I really appreciated it when my manager allowed me the time and schedule to do my work right. Later in my career, I found myself paying it forward by giving the same opportunity to those who worked for me.

DON'T MIX OPERATIONAL AND NON-OPERATIONAL TASKS

Operational tasks are the mission critical activities and department processes that, by definition, take precedence over all other department activities. In Information Technology (IT) groups, it's running the daily and nightly production. In Finance groups, it's opening and closing the monthly books, dealing with budgeting, and cash flow issues. In Human

Resources groups, it's salary planning, hiring new people, performance reviews, and dealing with unexpected employee related issues.

Non-operational tasks are everything else. This includes all of those things you would like to do within your department to move forward. This is project work, documentation, cleaning common office spaces, implementing new processes, other activities that help move your department forward.

If possible, you don't want to assign operational and non-operational tasks to the same person. The reason is that operational tasks, by design, have to come first. As a result, it becomes very difficult or impossible to ensure that your team's non-operational tasks can be completed on time. This is because it's very hard to know exactly how much of your team's efforts will be spent on production-related activities in a given day, week, or month.

For example, I spent many years managing IT groups. Given the nature of IT in most organizations, it's very common, and often a necessity, to have employees responsible for operational tasks and have various project related goals. The problem for the employees is that their project work often has many interruptions, stops, and starts because when production related issues occur, and their project work stops. The problem for me as the manager was that in addition to my production responsibilities, I was also responsible for meeting pre-defined deadlines on our project work. Production-related problems were extremely stressful, not only because of their high visibility and importance within the company, but also because it dramatically reduced the chances of my department meeting its deadlines.

My suggestion is that to the extent possible, divide your staff between those performing production-related tasks and those performing non-production related tasks.

If you are in the situation where your team members must be given both types of responsibilities, consider the following:

1. Work to improve your processes as much as possible to minimize the number and length of production-related interruptions.

2. Try to minimize the number of formalized project deadlines to people outside your department.

3. If you must give specified deadlines, overestimate their time-frames to properly account for production-related interruptions.

4. Keep a close eye on project progress and deadlines. The sooner you know that a project is falling behind, the more time you will have to make the appropriate adjustments.

5. Keep those you have commitments with continually informed on the progress of their projects and the amount of time your department is spending on operational activities. This transparency of project status and required production activities may minimize the political issues related to missing project deadlines.

Even under the best of circumstances, mixing operational and non-operational tasks is not ideal; however, with careful planning and reasonably stable operational processes, this scenario can be effectively managed.

MEETING TIMES BASED ON CIRCADIAN RHYTHMS

When are you most energetic, wide awake, and ready to take on the world? On the other side of that coin, when during the workday would you prefer to be taking a nap to recharge your internal batteries? Enough about you, when during the workday do you think your boss, staff, clients, customers, and peers are most awake or half asleep?

The answers to the previous questions can be of great value to you in regard to your staff's productivity, when negotiating with your peers and customers, and trying to get your boss to agree to a proposal that's near and dear to your heart.

The rationale behind this can best be described by explaining an old business trick. The trick is to negotiate a deal with someone when you are totally mentally awake and the person you are negotiating with is at slightly less than full capacity. No, I don't mean with alcohol or other mental recreational substances; I mean a delicious bowl of pasta and meatballs (actually one of my favorites).

Imagine this scenario: you bring your future client out to lunch at your favorite restaurant. Your future client, by your recommendation, orders a big bowl of pasta with turkey meatballs. Meanwhile, you decide to get a big salad with light dressing with the excuse that you're watching your weight. Then, right after the meal you start negotiating the contract. Guess who's wide awake and who's a little bit sleepy? Now, guess who will probably far better in the contract negotiation?

This story illustrates the advantage of knowing your daily mental cycles and the mental cycles of those around you. Listed below are a few practical applications of this technique:

» If you would like to have a very fruitful brainstorming session with your boss on an important business issue, then schedule the meeting at a time of day when both you and your boss are as mentally alert as possible.

» If you want to reduce your department's productivity loss associated with weekly staff meetings, have it at a time of day when your staff, on average, is less mentally alert, leaving their most productive time of day for work on important tasks.

» If you are negotiating with a business peer about who gets the office overlooking the ocean and one who gets the office overlooking the parking lot and the dumpsters, then schedule the meeting when you are most mentally alert and he/she is less focused. Alternatively, invite him/her out for a nice pasta lunch, as a treat. ☺

» If you are interviewing for a new job over lunch with a potential new employer, be very careful what you eat to assure you are on the top of your game. Maybe, even have a cup of coffee before you go.

» If you are obliged to attend committee meetings where you have no vested interest other than to make an appearance, then try to schedule the meetings when you are at your lowest mental strength during the workday.

» If you are giving an important presentation to upper management or a prospective client and want them fully engaged in the conversation, then try to schedule it at a time when you, the presenter, and they, the audience, are as sharp and cognitively alert as possible.

This concept/technique is by no mean foolproof, but it does have merit. My goal in teaching you this technique is not so you can take advantage of others. As seen in the above examples, (except of course, for the office facing the ocean) are ways that you can increase your team's work efficiency, maximize your personal productivity, and enhance your communication with others.

WORKING IN THE SHOWER CAN BE VERY PRODUCTIVE

As funny as it sounds, some of my best work ideas have come to me when I'm not at the office. As a software developer early in my career, there were times when I would practically be beating my head against my keyboard trying to define the best way to write a piece of software and then, have the perfect design pop into my head while watching a baseball game on TV that evening.

Later in my career, as I moved into the management ranks, I learned not only to take advantage of this phenomenon myself, but to also teach it to others on my team. Now, I would like to explain it to you. My disclaimer here is that I'm not a professional in this area of science. However, I did take a psychology class in high school in the early 1970s, but I don't think this makes me an expert.

Ok, here I go. When stressed, it's hard to have deep creative thought, at least for me. What I find is that when I am relaxed, it allows me to:

» Think about an issue with a fresh mind because of the time that elapsed since you first encountered the issue.

» Have your subconscious mind working on the issue when you are doing other things.

» Think more deeply about the topic and develop multiple potential solutions.

» Play mental gymnastics by comparing and contrasting these potential solutions.

The advantage of having the time to do the above is that it allows you to make decisions that are thoughtful, not knee-jerk based, develop the type of elegant and effective solutions that take time to mentally incubate and contemplate the pros and cons of each potential solution, which give you an understanding of the implications related to each.

This technique can work well for senior executives, new managers, and individual contributors. We all have problems that must be solved, decisions to make, and tasks to complete.

I use this technique of allowing myself relaxed time to make a decision whenever possible. In fact, when I'm pushed to make a very important decision quickly, unless speed is truly required, I'll say I want to sleep on it. This gives me the time to literally sleep on it, which having the evening to contemplate my potential options makes a more thoughtful (and usually better) decision. I use this technique when I decide which person to hire, to properly price when delivering custom training, how to best deal with a difficult employee issue, and countless other personal and professional decision points.

I have come up with great problem solving solutions in the shower, commuting to and from work, while making dinner (I love to cook), and in virtually every other setting that I find to be relaxing and undisturbed. Try this technique for yourself. You may also find it to be of great value when making important decisions. You may also find that taking the time to reflect before acting may save you from making mistakes that you will later regret.

KEY CHAPTER TAKEAWAYS

Maximize Productivity by Knowing Your Zone

» Teach this concept to your staff to help them maximize their productivity.

» Always assign tasks to each staff member related to all four levels, which allows them the flexibility to implement this time management strategy.

» When possible, provide appropriate lead time on deliverables to not force high level work during low level zone efficiency.

» Understanding the general times of day when your team members are not in their highest zones, which allows you to schedule meetings and other low-energy activities at appropriate times.

Managers, Knowledge Workers Work and Time Chunks

» Managers tend to work in 30 minute and 60 minute time frames.

» Knowledge workers tend to work in three hour time frames.

» When managers impose manager timeframes on knowledge workers creativity and productivity suffer.

Don't Mix Operational and Non-Operational Tasks

» Operational tasks are the mission critical activities and department processes that, by definition, take precedence over all other department activities.

» Non-operational tasks are everything else. It includes all of those things you would like to do within your department to move forward.

» If you can, use separate staff for operation and non-operational activities.

Meeting Times Based on Circadian Rhythms

»   Scheduling important meetings based on the time of day that you, your staff and others are at their best and worst mentally can be used to your advantage.

»   The trick is to negotiate a deal with someone when you are totally mentally awake and the person you are negotiating with is at slightly less than full capacity.

»   This concept/technique is by no mean foolproof, but it does have merit.

Working in the Shower Can be Very Productive

»   Reflecting on important issues when relaxed can help you make better decisions.

»   When relaxed, it can be easier to develop deep, innovative, and thoughtful solutions to difficult problems and challenges.

»   Taking the time to reflect before acting can potentially help you avoid doing things that you may later regret.

11. ONGOING PROCESS IMPROVEMENT

Discovering Small Gains That Make Big Wins

· · · · ·

> Nothing is less productive than to make more efficient what should not be done at all.
>
> **— *Peter Drucker***

I view ongoing process improvement like dropping pennies in a jar. Each penny, like each small improvement, seems to be of no value. However, at the end of the year when you look back at all the small changes that were made and compare your processes from a year ago to those today, you will see a vast improvement. This is how quality companies lower their costs, take advantage of economies of scale, compete with their competition, and increase their profits.

Enhancing business processes is an important and long-lasting way to increase organizational productivity. The reason is because processes are tasks, which are performed on an ongoing basis. Therefore, enhance the process once and benefit from its enhanced efficiency again and again. With that said, process enhancement should be viewed as both a short-term cost savings for today, and as a long term investment in your company's future profitability.

The process enhancement procedure can best be performed using the following five steps:

> "Process enhancement should be viewed as both a short-term cost savings for today and also as a long term investment in your company's future profitability."

1. Decide which process to enhance
2. Measure the current factors you wish to improve (i.e. time, cost, and etc.)
3. Enhance the process
4. Re-measure the factors you tried to improve
5. Report the value of the process enhancement

1. DECIDE WHICH PROCESS TO ENHANCE

When I looked back at the various processes I attempted to enhance over the years, I realized there were many reasons why those specific processes were selected. Those reasons are listed below. Take note that I'm using the word "transaction" loosely, simply to refer to a single iteration of the process.

» Productivity based reasons
  › Reduce the cost per transaction
  › Reduce the time to process each transaction
  › Reduce the amount of human interaction per transaction
» Technological based reasons
  › Fix software bugs
  › Replace an old technology with a newer one
» Business based reasons
  › Better alignment with existing corporate goals

> › Due to a change in corporate direction
>
> › Due to an increase in transaction volume
>
> » Legal or regulatory reasons
>
> › Change in federal or state law
>
> › Change in compliance-based regulations

While reviewing these reasons, you will see that most of them are not productivity related, but instead are for technological, business, legal, or regulatory purposes. The trick is that if you are modifying a process for non-productivity purposes, then you should also try to enhance its productivity. This tactic is similar to the old automobile adage "Since we have the hood of the car open anyway, we might as well check the oil while we're here." For technological and business type modifications, adding a productivity type dimension has the potential to enhance the project's ROI (Return on Investment).

For legal and regulatory type process modifications, the advantage of this approach is that it allows you to add some business value to your projects. While it is, of course, very important to follow the law and regulatory requirements, these types of activities provide no additional business advantage, generally speaking.

The next question that comes to mind is, given so many reasons to update a process, how do you choose which process enhancement is most important? I'm sorry to say there is no magic algorithm that can be used on all projects for all companies and in all

> *"Develop a culture where productivity enhancement is, by default, always considered a part of process improvement."*

industries. The best advice I can give you here is to trust your judgement and your management's judgement. Also, try to develop a culture where productivity enhancement is by default always considered a part of process improvement.

2. MEASURE THE CURRENT FACTORS YOU WISH TO IMPROVE

The reason you want to measure the cost, time or other factors you wish to improve before modifying the process is because you can use them as a benchmark to assess the level of improvement upon project completion.

There is an old IBM advertisement which depicts the importance of process measurement about fifteen years ago. The premise was that a person runs into his boss's office all excited that he saved the company a nickel. His boss says, "Big deal, so what if you saved the company five cents, we are a billion dollar company." Then the employee answers by saying, "You don't understand, I just saved a nickel per transaction on five hundred thousand transactions a day!"

The story was not only a fun advertisement for a product I can't recall, but it was also an enormously powerful example of why you should properly measure the processes performed within your department.

When measuring the processes within your department, consider the various types of statistics including those listed below. Of course, not all of these measurements are applicable to all processes, but this list should give you a good idea of the types of measurements that may be applicable to the work done within your department:

» Number of times each task/process is performed per week.

» How long each task/process takes to perform.

» The average pay of the people performing each task.

» The cost of materials and/or other costs incurred by each task.

» The value associated with each completed task/item to your company.

These measurements allow you to calculate these types of statistics that allow you to assess the business value of each task your department performs:

» The total time spent within your department on each process.

» The value and/or return on investment of the process to the company.

» Which processes within your department take the most time and/ or cost the most money.

This last item is also incredibly important because it helps you prior-itize your time on which processes should be streamlined. For example, let's say your department performs two types of tasks. Process #1 takes three hours to complete, but if redesigned, the time could be reduced to two hours. Process #2 takes on average forty-five minutes to perform, but the time could be reduced to thirty-five minutes, if the process was redesigned. Which process do you improve first? At first glance, you may say process #1. With that said, to answer the question correctly there are a few other items you need to consider:

» The number of times each process is performed per week

» The average pay grades of the people performing each process

» If one of the processes is a bottleneck causing issues within other departments

» The level of effort and expense needed to streamline each process

With the above information in hand, you can then statistically build a business case as to which process should be improved first. In addition to the obvious advantage of this type of analysis, this empirical evidence also has an advantage for you personally. This advantage is that you can precisely quantify the amount of time and money your work is saving the company. Think of it this way, which of the following two state-ments would you like to be able to say to your boss during your annual performance review?

1. Over the past year, I think I saved the company a lot of money im-proving some of our department processes.

2. This year, I saved the company $325,000 by streamlining two of my department's processes. The first process saved $200,000 in

labor costs and the second process saved $125,000 in transaction costs. Even better, looking forward over the next five years, this will be a savings to the company of $1,625,000.

The first statement may sound nice, but the second statement will help get you promoted.

3. ENHANCE THE PROCESS

The key to a successful process improvement project is the same for all projects; management support, adequate resources, a clear objective, competent leadership, and a quality staff. Regardless of your professional vocation or future professional aspirations, if you don't have a strong management background, it would be well worth your while to gain these skills.

4. RE-MEASURE THE FACTORS YOU TRIED TO IMPROVE

Re-measuring the factors you tried to improve has three primary functions; operational, political, and educational. Operationally, it allows you to create new departmental benchmarks to be used for scheduling, budgeting, and planning purposes. Politically, it can be used to illustrate your successful leadership and/or innovative abilities with the goal of future financial or organizational gain. Lastly, educationally, it allows you to look back closely at your work for lessons learned that can be used to enhance your success on future projects. Because of its importance to organizational advancement, this concept of re-measurement is found virtually all process improvement methodologies, such as Six Sigma.

5. REPORT THE VALUE OF THE PROCESS ENHANCEMENT

Since my professional move from corporate executive to leadership trainer and keynote speaker, I've asked my audience two questions:

1. Before beginning a new project at work, are you required to estimate its value to the company via a Return on Investment (ROI) calculation or other similar metrics?

2. For those of you who raised your hand, after the project is completed, do you then go back and assess if the project actually provided the value that was used to initially approve it?

When I asked the first question, usually about 60% of the audience raised their hand. However, when I asked the second question, only about 10% kept their hand raised.

My questions to you are the same. If you answered "no" to the first question, then you should define these measurements and estimates just for yourself. Then, calculate the value of your efforts, at project end.

The reason to calculate and report this value ties back to the IBM story I told you earlier in this chapter. Remember, if you can't calculate and quantify it, then it's much harder for you and your team to get credit for a job well done. Also, remember that Step 6 of the Productivity Pyramid is the reinvestment of the time, money and resources harvested from your productivity improvement projects. Proper measurement is a crucial component of the reinvestment process.

Lastly, with your project complete, the results measured and the harvested time, money and resources redeployed, don't forget to document your project process, challenges and successes to facilitate Step 7 of the Productivity Pyramid, "Productivity Project Reiteration."

KEY CHAPTER TAKEAWAYS

The process enhancement procedure is:

1. Decide which process to enhance
2. Measure the current factors you wish to improve (i.e. time, cost, and etc.)
3. Enhance the process
4. Re-measure the factors you tried to improve
5. Report the value of the process enhancement

12. ASSET REUSE

Solving the puzzle of buying/building it once and using it again and again

● ● ● ● ●

> The key to reusing your Intellectual Property is to look at it holistically in regard to its value, quality and applicability to other business challenges.
>
> *— Eric P. Bloom*

At a high level, asset reuse is the repurposing of intellectual property, software, physical devices, business processes, and other similar company assets. From my perspective, this is the most powerful and valuable of the seven productivity amplifiers. I say this because it helps you get more value out of the items you already own. In effect, you're getting additional value for free.

Economically, there is a major financial incentive to reuse your created, purchased, and acquired assets. As an example, let's assume that the purchase of a new expensive

> *"Asset reuse is the repurposing of intellectual property, software, physical devices, business processes, and other similar company assets.*

machine costing $50,000 was justified based on its ability to save the company $60,000 (For the finance people reading this, yes, I'm totally ignoring the time value of money to make the example as simple as possible.) over a machine's expected life of three years. Therefore, its return on investment is 20% = ((60,000 – 50,000) / 50,000).

If the machine can be used for a second purpose that saves an additional $5,000 during its three year expected life, then the total return on investment of the machine becomes 30% = ((65,000 – 50,000) / 50,000).

This increase from 20% to 30% was caused by the increased return (the $5,000) with no change in the amount invested (the $50,000).

The key to maximizing your asset reuse potential is to follow the six steps process listed:

1. Create an asset inventory
2. Categorize and combine assets into logical groups
3. Assess asset reuse potential
4. Gain approval
5. Implement reuse plan
6. Measure results

1. CREATE AN ASSET INVENTORY:

When performing this first step of finding and inventorying your assets, you possibly will be surprised by the number of assets you actually have, the number of potential candidates for reuse, and the value this single step provides.

By the term "asset", I mean anything that you have purchased, created, or acquired. By purchased, it could be software, trucks, medical devices, or any other tangible/conceptual items. By created, I'm referring to internally created software, whitepapers, marketing materials, training materials,   etc. Lastly, by acquired, I'm referring to opt-in email lists, customers, website traffic, and other similar items.

The reason for this broad definition is that with enough ingenuity almost anything can be repurposed. For example, farm tractors purchased to assist in planting and harvesting can be leased to construction and/ or landscaping companies during the growing season as an additional source of income. Another example, a great piece of internally developed software by your IT department may be a great cloud-based product that could be offered on the internet a new source of company revenue.

The examples are endless and will become more apparent in the steps that follow:

Lastly, as part of this asset inventorying process, you should take note of any specific assets that cannot be used in certain ways. For example, if your customer private statement says you will keep their information confidential, then you can't legally sell their information to other companies. However, you may be able to perform high-level analytics on this data and sell the aggregate results and/or analytical findings.

2. CATEGORIZE AND COMBINE ASSETS INTO LOGICAL GROUPS:

With all your assets listed, your next step is to categorize them into logical groups based on asset type and logical groupings.

By asset type, I'm referring to its physical, or logical makeup. For example, a list of all published research documents could be a subset of all written materials. Other written assets that could be subcategorized in this way are marketing collateral, training materials, paper-based client assessments, and website content.

By logical groupings, I'm referring to various asset types related to a single activity, such as inventory control. The process may employ various logical and physical items including inventory software, barcode writers, barcode readers, RFID readers, fork lifts, portable storage bins, inventory procedure manuals, and custom designed inventory tag software.

3. Assess reuse potential:

Now that you have all your assets identified and categorized, the magic can begin. Your next step is to brainstorm with other parts of your company on how these assets can be used to solve new problems, improve existing processes, create new products, or establish new revenue sources. When considering their potential reuse potential, consider the following potential roadblocks:

» Legal

» Vendor licensing agreements

» Legal and regulatory requirements

» Contractual obligations on how specified equipment can be used

» Safety

» Concerns related to using equipment outside its intended use

» Political

» Internal owner's willingness to share their assets

» Ability to effectively work across organizational silos

» Support

» Additional costs related to incremental usage

» Ability to provide internal support to new asset usage

Continuing on the first example in step #2, the published research papers could be combined into a new online product offering. The paper-based assessment could be converted into an online tool and used as the first step in a consulting process, followed by onsite consulting, training, and executive coaching.

Let's now continue the second example from step #2, related to the warehouse items. The question to be asked is "Where else in the company could an inventory-related solution be of value? The inventory system, barcode writers, and barcode readers could be used by the Technology Help Desk to track employee laptops, tablets, cell phones, printers, and other related items. Additionally, items such as printer cartridges can be affixed with RFID cards before being placed in inventory closets. Then the periodic physical inventory counts can be performed via the RFID readers, versus by hand. Because the inventory software, barcode writers/readers and RFID readers are already owned by the company, the only out-of-pocket expense related to this scenario is the minimal cost of the RFID chips.

4. GAIN APPROVAL:

With your idea in hand and business partner secured, your next step is to gain approval for the project. Certainly the approval process for this project itself should be based on the same criteria as other projects within your company, but this one has some additional points of interest:

» The potential Return on Investment (ROI) will be much greater because the assets being used are already owned by the company.

» Remember to define project's Critical Success Factors (CSFs)

» Remember to define project's Expected Productivity Gains (EPGs)

Take note that if this is the first repurposing project of its kind, it may receive significant senior management visibility as a model for future reuse type projects.

5. IMPLEMENT REUSE PLAN:

There isn't too much for me to say on this one. Of course, your goal is to implement your reuse vision in cooperation with your reuse partner. Also, remember to keep your project's Critical Success Factors (CSFs) and Expected Productivity Gains (EPGs) in mind. This information will help you position your project for success and provide a basis as to how the project will be measured once completed.

6. Measure results:

Measurement was discussed at length with the Productivity Pyramid discussion, so I won't repeat it here. However, I will pass along a few additional thoughts.

If this is your first reuse project of this type:

» Take great pains to assure you properly capture all of the project's costs and benefits. This will allow you to take full credit for the project's productivity gains.

» Document the process you used to define and capture the project's costs and benefits. This process can be used as a template for future reuse related projects.

Also, if the project, is productivity enhancing, please remember to include the regained "opportunity cost" discussed earlier in the book.

Lastly, keep a log of the measurements of all reuse projects for future analysis. It may help you develop benchmarks related to the ROI of this type of project. Additionally, it may prove interesting to compare the ROI of these projects to the ROI of standard projects (non-reuse), which are required to create new assets from scratch, versus repurposing existing resources.

Key Chapter Takeaways

The key to maximizing your asset reuse potential is to follow the six steps listed below.

1. Create an asset inventory.

2. Categorize and combine assets into logical groups.

3. Assess asset reuse potential.

4. Gain approval.

5. Implement reuse plan.

6. Measure results.

13. KNOWLEDGE STORAGE AND TRANSFER

Organizational learning at its best

* * * * *

A candle never loses it light when it lights another candle.

— Father James Keller

I heard a story about how an oil company used a discussion board in a very innovative way to transfer corporate knowledge across the generations. I don't know if this story is true; however, it illustrates knowledge transfer so well that I'm going to tell it anyway.

As the older oil well engineers began to retire, it became evident that younger engineers didn't know how to perform proper maintenance and repair of the older oil rigs, some of which had been in service for thirty or forty years. Even though the younger engineers could eventually figure out how to perform the needed work, the learning curve dramatically reduced their productivity and hurt their oil field output.

As you may expect, this became a major issue for the oil company. To solve the problem the company created a discussion board, then gave access (and a monthly stipend) to a select group of knowledgeable retired engineers and to currently active employed workers in the oil fields. When a younger engineer had a question on how to properly service a specific oil rig, he would post a question on the discussion board. The retired engineers, potentially sitting on a beach a thousand miles away, would answer the post. This simple process had the following benefits:

» Increased engineer productivity by reducing the learning curve on how to maintain older oil rigs.

» Because the discussion board content was permanently stored and categorized by rig, it recaptured and documented lost corporate knowledge.

» Reduced operational risk via the ability to tap into their retired brain trust as technical issues occurred.

This discussion board concept can also be used as an internal company communication and documentation tool. The only difference would be that knowledgeable active employees, rather than retirees, would be answering the posted questions.

As this story illustrates, , knowledge management can generate great dividends. Newly hired employees must learn the company's culture, processes, and politics. Existing

> *"Knowledge management can generate great productivity dividends."*

employees who are transferred to new roles or promoted must quickly come up to speed on their new responsibilities. New company products and services must be quickly understood by the salesforce in order to be sold.

When you think about corporate knowledge, divide it into three categories; creation, retention, and distribution. The sections will outline how these categories of corporate knowledge can be used to help drive organizational growth and productivity:

KNOWLEDGE CREATION

Knowledge Creation refers to employee growth through performing work-related tasks, general professional experiences, and corporate training.

Work-related tasks include the creation of:

» New products and services.

» Implementation of innovative business, technical, or manufacturing processes.

» Research of all types.

» Documentation of all types including, marketing, sales, and technical.

» Business presentations.

» Computer software.

These types of activities enhance corporate knowledge in two ways: First, the employees performing the tasks enhance their topical knowledge and skill sets. Second, the intellectual property they are creating becomes an asset of the company that can be used in perpetuity to increase revenue, reduce costs, and as the basis for more advanced future creations.

In the long run, one of the most valuable assets of mature organizations is the corporate knowledge embodied in their products, processes, and the people who oversee their daily processing.

General professional experiences are the work-based victories and failures that employees encounter on a daily basis. Each of these wins and losses teaches a lesson on how things should and should not be done within their work environment. These experiences weed out the employees not yet ready for promotion and accelerate the upward mobility of those who are ready to take on new and more advanced challenges.

Corporate training can either be a true accelerant of corporate knowledge, or a noncontributory factor; based on the organization's culture, size of the training budget, and employee interest in attending offered classes. If the organization's culture recognizes the value of training, managers with take training seriously and assure their employees are properly trained. Without it, even the best designed classes will remain unattended. Like all business initiatives, funding is both an illustration of corporate priority and the vehicle through which activities, such as training are enabled, without it, the best intentions will wither on the vine. Lastly, if the employees have no interest and see no value in learning new skills, then even the most heavily supported and well budgeted training initiatives will fall on deaf ears and provide no value.

I tend to break training classes into three types: compulsory, hard skills and soft skills.

Compulsory training is required by law, industry regulated bodies or professional licensing groups. All too often these classes are viewed by senior management and the employees who are required to participate as more of a task to be completed than an opportunity to gain new skills. However, if these classes are provided in an engaging and creative way, then there is real potential for them to enhance organizational knowledge and help propel employee growth. If this "value-add" can be achieved, then it conceptually transforms its cost of the training from an expense of doing business, to an investment in the company's future.

Hard skills training is the term used to define task-related training such as computer programming, laboratory techniques, equipment operation, and computer software training. These types of training classes are generally taken by individual contributors as a way to enhance their current job skills, or prepare them to perform additional tasks. These types of training classes have the company benefits of:

» Increasing employee productivity through the use of newly

learned techniques

» Reduced attrition due to employee feeling of continued professional growth

» Expanding the company's technical knowledge base and skills level

For the employee, hard skills have the benefit of enhancing marketability and professional growth.

Soft skill training refers to instruction in leadership and interpersonal communication. This type of training is of value to all employees, from the newest college intern to the most experienced CEO. While this information can be said to generally increase the company's overall knowledge base, from a productivity perspective, its real power is in helping the organizations drive their success through competent leadership and by spreading internally acquired knowledge to all those within the company.

It's been my experience that most companies agree that training is an important component of workforce productivity, talent management, employee morale, and company competitiveness. The questions arise over what type of training to provide, who gets it and how much company time and money can be used to procure it. There is an old joke that training is both an employee right and a privilege. The employee generally thinks it's his right. His/her manager generally thinks that it's a privilege.

KNOWLEDGE RETENTION

Knowledge Retention is the process of permanently storing corporate knowledge within documents, social media platforms, business process, and the company's internal consciousness.

Of course, document sharing is a necessity of business life. The trick is to store the documents in a way that they can be efficiently retrieved. As a friend of mine likes to say "A document repository should be more like a blender than a disposal. With a blender, the ingredients go in and an organized result can be retrieved. With a disposal, you put the ingredients in and they can never be retrieved."

> *"Knowledge Retention is the process of permanently storing corporate knowledge within documents, social media platforms, business process, and the company's internal consciousness."*

Below are a number of document sharing tips:

- » Ensure proper security is in place related to who can see which documents.

- » Define file name conventions (standards) to make it easier to find related documents.

- » Assign a document administrator to help coordinate the storage and retrieval of documents. This may seem like an unneeded overhead function, but it will help keep your document repository consistent, usable, and retrievable.

- » Make it easy for people to use; otherwise, people will avoid using it.

- » Assign meta tags (searchable key words that describe the document's content) to each document.

- » Assign an author's name to each document so readers can follow up with the author, if he/she has follow up questions.

- » Have a versioning feature that allows you to store multiple revisions of the same document. Otherwise, people will begin using their own naming conventions and unnecessarily expand the number of documents contained within your repository.

- » Periodically, email the document authors a list of the documents they stored within the repository with the request to delete unneeded and obsolete files. This will reduce the overall size of the repository, prevent people from retrieving out-of-date documents, and making it easier to find needed information.

From a social media perspective, in addition to discussion boards previously discussed in the oil company story at the beginning of the chapter, wikis are also a great way to capture and retain corporate knowledge. My definition of an internal company wiki is text that describes one or more of the following:

» What something is

» How something can be used

» How to do something

In essence, it's documentation written by one employee to be used in the future by many others. I like to think of it as a way to capture corporate knowledge for the benefit of the company's future. When an employee writes a wiki, unless instructed to as part of his/her job, it's a very selfless act. The employee writing the wiki obviously knows the material being written. Therefore, the fact that it's documented is of no real value to the writer. With that said, writing the wiki can actually be a productivity enhancer to the writer if it's the answer to a commonly asked question that can be referenced online, versus by calling the writer.

A company's internal consciousness is a combination of the organization's culture, problem solving processes, competitive spirit, and overall business philosophy. This is not a specific type of knowledge per se; it's about the way the company gets things done. This is the resonance of the company's founders, former management, and current leadership. This historical echo, blended with a current day mentality, is what converts a group of people working together to a business entity with a life of its own. With long-lasting companies and the leadership changes, the workforce comes and

> *"A company's internal consciousness is a combination of the organization's culture, problem solving processes, competitive spirit, and overall business philosophy."*

goes, yet the company remains. This seemingly living entity is built on the shoulders of its collective corporate knowledge.

KNOWLEDGE DISTRIBUTION

The creation of corporate knowledge is a great beginning. The retention of knowledge is a great next step. It's the distribution and use of this knowledge that maximizes its value to the organization. Knowledge Distribution is the transfer of knowledge from one employee to another via training, mentoring, webinars, videos, and instructional documentation.

As described earlier in this chapter, there are many ways to create and retain organizational knowledge. The true value of this collective thought is how it's used to move the company forward. One of the most powerful and permanent ways to take advantage of this collected corporate knowledge is by building it into usable business processes, which in effect, convert this knowledge into usable action.

When new processes become operational, the work that went into designing them begin to pay productivity-based dividends in perpetuity. Until I started Manager Mechanics in 2009, I had always worked for medium or large companies that had been in existence for many years. What I had not realized during my many years employed within "Corporate America" was the time, effort, experimentation, successes, failures, and innovative process that went into creating the organization's internal processes. I just took them for granted because they already existed. Each one of these processes at some previous point in time was a new innovation created through the ingenuity, knowledge, and hard work of others, many of whom were no longer employed by the company. From a knowledge retention perspective, these processes are the embodiment of the collective expertise, experience, and creativity of exited employees. In many ways, this is the ideal way to maximize the return on investment of knowledge creation and retention because it's the gift that keeps on giving, as the expression goes.

There is also great value in transferring knowledge and knowhow from employee to employee. This transferred expertise, which gives multiple people the same expertise simultaneously protects the company from knowledge losses due to attrition and provides assignment flexibility because multiple people can perform the same task. Techniques that facilitate this information cross-pollination include the following:

» Employee Onboarding.

» Employee cross-training.

» Job rotation.

» Job shadowing.

» Internal coaching and mentorship programs.

» Task video libraries.

» Discussion board and wikis (previously discussed).

» Procedural manuals.

» "Brown bag" lunch training sessions.

» Recorded internal instructional webinars.

» Mastermind groups.

EMPLOYEE ONBOARDING

When a new person is hired into your group, you're job as the manager has just begun. Remember, if you made the decision to hire this person, his/her success or failure at the company is an illustration of your decision-making ability and your competency as a manager. With that said, it's in your best interest to help assure the success of your new employee. From a knowledge transfer perspective, the list of below activities can help your new employee quickly come up to speed on department/company processes, become properly acclimated to the company, begin formulating a good reputation, and stay clear of numerous pitfalls that can accidently derail a new employee's potential achievements.

1. Give the employee a "department orientation". That is to say, schedule a meeting during his/her first day of work and spend an hour or two one-on-one with the employee. This meeting will give you the opportunity to get to know the new employee a little better, answer any questions that he/she has about the job, and, from a knowledge transfer perspective, provide him/her with detailed information on the company, your department, their job, and your expectations regarding their future performance. During this meeting, consider explaining the following:

   a. The company in general.

   b. Your department's role within the company.

   c. All the processes your department performs, including those processes outside the new employee's job description/function.

   d. A little background on each person in your department, including their job function, longevity with the company, and any generally known points of interest.

   e. A little insight into department and company politics.

   f. A detailed explanation of his/her specific job function, responsibilities, your expectations as his/her manager.

   g. A detailed explanation of how to perform his/her job.

   h. Background on internal company departments, vendors, clients, and others that he/she will be working with as part of his/her job.

   i. Schedule a follow-up meeting two or three days after the "department orientation" meeting and instruct the new employee to keep track of any questions he/she may come up with during his/her few days of work as a basis for discussion during the follow up meeting.

2. Give the employee the "office tour". That is to say, walk the new employee around the office showing him/her where things are

(rest rooms, supply cabinet, coffee machine, and etc.) This will save the new person from having to introduce himself/herself to people by asking, "Hi, I'm new here. Will you please point me toward the restroom?"

3. Give the employee the "walk around". That is to say, walk the new employee around the office introducing him/her to the other employees in your group. This will allow him/her to begin associating people's names and faces.

4. Create a formalized "buddy system" between the new employee and an existing employee within your department. Have the existing employee act as a mentor to the new employee until he/she is up to speed on all aspects of his/her job. This formalized mentoring gives the new employee a specific person to learn from and ask questions of without feeling like a nudge or a bother.

5. The "follow-up orientation meeting" (scheduled during your initial employee orientation meeting) provides the new employee the opportunity to ask you questions based on his/her first few days of work. It also provides you the opportunity to provide any constructive feedback that is required based on your observation or comments made by others.

Following the above steps is, of course, not a guarantee that your new employees will succeed and prosper; however, it is giving your newly hired employees a great head start and the knowledge base needed to minimize their learning curve and maximize their future productivity.

> "Employee Onboarding gives newly hired employees a great head start and the knowledge base needed to minimize their learning curve and maximize their future productivity."

EMPLOYEE CROSS-TRAINING

The term "Cross Training" refers to the practice of teaching the people in your group how to perform the jobs/tasks of other people in your group. For example, say you are the manager of a grocery store and have two people working for you. One of your employees, "Bill", knows how to stock the shelves. The other person, "Mary", knows how to work the cash register. Teaching Mary to do Bill's job and Bill how to do Mary's job is considered cross training.

Cross training is a win-win for both you and your team members. From your perspective as the manager, if one person leaves your group or just simply goes on vacation, then you have someone else who knows how to do the job. From the employee's perspective and using the example above, both Mary and Bill have learned new skills which make them more valuable to the company (good for you) and more professionally marketable (good for them).

There are two primary ways to cross train people: on-the-job training only and on-the-job training supplemented with formalized education. The decision to include formalized training is a function of the:

- » Complexity of the task.
- » Business or legal requirement.
- » Employee's transferable knowledge to the new task.
- » Budget to pay for the class.
- » Employee's willingness to be cross trained.
- » Enough time to concentrate on cross training.
- » Ability of the cross trainer to explain what he/she is doing and ability of the cross trainee to learn the new job.

I have found that cross training works the best when people are willing and able to teach and learn the new material and they have the time to do so. Your job as manager is to assure that you are cross training the right people (have the want and ability) and that you are providing them the time and atmosphere to learn. If your team members feel pressured and overworked to get their regular tasks done, cross training will never happen.

JOB ROTATION

Job rotation is the process of systematically moving employees from job to job with the specific intent of widening their experience to prepare them for future promotional opportunities. As great as this sounds, for it to work effectively the company's internal culture must see job laterals as a means of future promotion, not as a way of languishing at the same organizational level.

Early in a person's career, say when they first enter the workforce after graduating college, job rotation as part of a corporate training program is viewed as wonderful way to gain the knowledge and skills needed to move ahead professionally. For those with many years of experience, all too often expanding horizontally is viewed as "not up; therefore, not of value".

From an employee perspective, job rotation can enhance employee strength in many ways:

» Perspective - by doing different types of job.

» Depth - from a wider range of experiences.

» Morale – by getting to try new things.

» Growth – by gaining new skills.

» Flexibility – by learning to adapt to new situations.

This widened employee experience provides management with the opportunity to redeploy these knowledgeable employees as necessity requires and as promotional openings occur.

JOB SHADOWING

By its name, job shadowing may sound mysterious or secretive, at first glance. Well, sorry, it's not. Job shadowing is the process of observing someone in the workplace with the specific goal of trying to understand what they do. Classically, job shadowing is used by students as a way of learning about a profession they are considering studying in school and potentially pursuing as their future livelihood. Take note, that this technique also can be used extremely effectively within the workplace and a low cost training tool in the following ways.

To TEACH JOB CANDIDATES ABOUT THE TASKS THEY WILL BE PERFORMING IF HIRED

Using job shadowing as a component of hiring has three major advantages: First, it gives the job candidate a chance to see what life will be like in the workplace on a daily basis if he/she decides to accept the job. Second, it gives the company a chance to see the candidate within the workplace and can gain a better understanding of his/her ability to perform the job if hired. Third, it allows both the candidate and the company to see if there is a personality fit.

To TEACH NEW EMPLOYEES HOW TO PERFORM STANDARDIZED TASKS

All too often, new employees don't receive the amount of training they need to get up to speed quickly on the new tasks they must perform. One main reason for this training deficiency is that other people in the department don't have the time to properly train newcomers to the group because they are too busy doing their own work. Because by definition, job shadowing is watching someone else do their job, the new employee can learn by watching while the experienced employee is getting his/her work done. Of course, there is the potential that questions from the new recruit may slow down the experienced person, but this question/answer dialog will be less disruptive for the experienced person than putting his/her work aside to provide formalized on-the-job instruction.

To TEACH NEW TASKS TO EXISTING EMPLOYEES AS PART OF A JOB ROTATION PROGRAM

This concept is similar to the one mentioned above, except instead of trying to train a newly hired employee, you are trying to train an existing employee how to perform a new task. The reason that job shadowing can work well as a cross training tool is because by requiring the employee to watch the task and to do the task, it indirectly gives him/her permission to not be immediately functionally productive, thus allowing him/her to gain an understanding of the job before being thrown into the fray to do it themselves.

To teach customer service people how their customers use the company's products

Using job shadowing as a way to enhance the company's external client service could almost be called, "A day in the life of your customer training." The concept here is that the better your customer service and/or technical support staff understand what the customer does with your product, the better job they can do providing assistance to your client base. For example, let's say you work for a software company that provides accounting software to doctors' offices. The better your technical support staff understands how a doctor's office works, the better they can explain how it should be used.

To teach internal service providers about the internal departments they are supporting

This use of job shadowing is similar to the one mentioned above, but in this case, the people being helped are inside, versus outside the company. This distinction not only allows the people in one department to better serve another department, but from a company perspective, it can greatly enhance the efficiency of inter-department company processes. For example, let's say step #1 of a company's billing process is performed by the Shipping Department and step #2 is done by the Accounting Office, based on the paperwork received from Shipping. If the people working in Shipping have a general understanding of how the paperwork is processed within Accounting, they can better complete this paperwork in a way that facilitates proper processing by the accountants. Conversely, if the people in Accounting have a general understanding of the shipping process, they can provide meaningful suggestions as to how the paperwork can be designed in a way that minimizes the Shipping Department's paperwork and simultaneously maximizes the Accounting Department's efficiency.

TO HELP EMPLOYEES EXPLORE ALTERNATIVE FUTURE CAREER OPTIONS

Lastly, this use of job shadowing is very similar to its original, and more traditional, definition. The difference here is that you are helping your employees, versus students, make informed career decisions on the future direction of their professional life.

As a manager, consider job shadowing as one of the many tools you use when training new employees, working to enhance your organization's effectiveness, and when helping those in your group navigate their careers. The beauty of this technique is that it's low cost, easy to administer, and can be highly effective.

COACHING AND MENTORING

As a manager, I believe you are not only responsible for the wellbeing of your department and its role within the company at large, but you are also responsible, if not legally then morally, to help the members of your staff grow professionally, and in some cases personally. As their leader, you are a figure of authority in their life. They may love you. They may hate you. Hopefully, they respect you.

If you are a history buff, you may be interested to know that the origin of the word "Mentor" is from Greek mythology. Mentor was a friend of Odysseus who asked him to nurture his foster brother when he left for the Trojan War. As a result, the word "mentor" historically came to mean a trusted advisor. Of course not all of your staff members may want you as a trusted advisor, but for those that will listen, it could be of advantage to you both.

The best managers I had in my career also acted as mentors and teachers to me, and other staff members. They taught me many valuable lessons related to technical topics, office politics, management processes, such as writing a good performance review, making presentations, and in some cases to be a better person, both professionally and personally.

Understand, that as a manager, being a good mentor to your staff members is not totally altruistic. It's also good for your department, your company, and you personally. Let's begin with how mentoring your staff is good for them.

Mentoring your staff provides them with the opportunity to learn from your wisdom, experience, mistakes, and general insights. Have you ever said to yourself "Wow, if I knew then what I know now?" Well guess what, in many cases you now know what in ten years your team members will wish they knew then. Why not give them a head start? This is mentoring.

Mentoring your team is good for your company for the following reasons:

» It increases the knowledge and ability of your staff.

» It increases the loyalty of your staff to you, and as a result to the company. Remember the old expression, "People join companies and leave managers."

» It helps your department run more effectively, thus helping company operations in general.

» IT helps you improve professionally. Remember, you are an employee also.

Mentoring your team is good for you for the following reasons:

» At a human level, it feels good to be helping other people.

» It builds loyalty in your staff toward you.

» It lowers you team's attrition rate, thus saving you from having to hire and train new staff.

» As you get an internal reputation of being a good manager, it will be easier for you to find and hire internal candidates.

» If your staff is happy and your department is running well, then it may assist you in getting a promotion.

» By mentoring and teaching others, you will find that you will gain new insights and deepen your skills.

TASK VIDEO LIBRARIES

Many forward thinking companies are using short employee made videos to teach other employees how to perform discreet tasks. For example, there is an insurance company that inspects the buildings it insures with the goal of making the buildings safer, which reduces the number of claims it has to pay. In this scenario, everyone wins.

To perform this inspection process, employees of the insurance company are sent to a building to inspect all its valves, gages, fire alarm systems, and other related equipment. As part of this process, if a video on how to perform the task doesn't exist, they video the testing process via the camera on their cell phone and add it to the corporate library. Then, when other employees go to inspect the building, they have video based instructions on how to perform the various tasks.

PROCEDURAL MANUALS

Procedural manuals may sound old and mundane, but if written well and updated as needed, they are a great mechanism to pass information from the author to those needing to acquire the author's knowledge.

To the author, writing this type of document may seem very time consuming and with no real personal return on invested time. There are two ways, however, that the author can gain value from this type of document creation: First, if the document is widely distributed and heavily used, it brings fame and prestige to the person who wrote it. Second, it may save the author from receiving endless calls on how to perform the tasks contained within the manual, thus, in the long-term, saving the author time.

"BROWN BAG" LUNCH TRAINING SESSIONS

For those not familiar with the term "brown bag", it refers to bringing your own lunch to the meetings. This type of training session is generally done at no cost to the company and is a great way to stretch your training budget. The speakers, versus being professional trainers, could be an executive within the company, a vendor describing a new product line or an employee describing a new technology, process, methodology, or other topic of interest.

This type of informal training session also has another big advantage. It's a speaking/presenting training ground for employees to practice the presentation skills in front of forgiving and supportive audiences. Depending on the presenter's current ability, sessions of this type can help the presenter feel more comfortable speaking in public, how to design

> *"This type of informal training session also has another big advantage. It's a speaking/presenting training ground for employees to practice the presentation skills in front of forgiving and supportive audiences."*

well-formed presentations, and other similar lessons that only practice in the spotlight can provide.

It's a wonderful thing, new knowledge for your team, improved presentation skills for the speaker and no cost to the company. With that said, if you have a few budget dollars, be a sport and bring in pizza, or a nice dessert.

INTERNAL INSTRUCTIONAL WEBINARS

A more advanced version of brown bag lunches as a way to distribute internal knowledge is a live webinar series using internal company executives, thought leaders and subject matter experts. In addition to being live, they should also be recorded and provided on demand to all company employees.

RECORDED INTERNAL INFORMATIONAL VIDEOS

These recorded webinars can come from many sources:

» Filmed internal training sessions.

» Executive presentations originally given at client conferences.

» Product marketing videos.

» Executives describing their business function specifically for this purpose.

» Descriptions of important internal technologies, products and/or processes given by internal subject matter experts specifically for this purpose.

» Filmed brown bag lunch presentations.

» Recorded internal webinars previously discussed.

Once created, these videos can be used company-wide at no cost since your company owns the content.

PEER GROUPS

A peer group is a collection of six to eight people at a similar organizational level or in a similar profession who meet on an ongoing basis to help each other professionally and for the good of the company. For example, having the SVPs of Marketing within six divisions of the same corporation meeting monthly to discuss marketing trends and provide each other advice on business related issues. Another example, five of the company's most experienced Java computer programmers meeting monthly to discuss best practices, programming techniques, and technical trends. These types of internal peer groups have three main advantages. First, peer groups allow talented groups of employees to learn from each other. This type of peer-learning within a company is of great value because it's done within the context of the work being performed, as opposed to general knowledge learned in a generic training class that must then be mentally synthesized into a usable business context. Second, as participants get to know each other's job roles, and they can give meaningful advice to each other related to current issues and future strategies. Not only does this create higher quality output, is only helps facilitate internal consistency across business functions. Lastly, as these high quality employees become friends, they will be less likely to leave the company because of the personal relationships they have created.

KEY CHAPTER TAKEAWAYS

» Discussion boards are a great way to simultaneously transfer knowledge from employee to employee and permanently collect it for future reference.

» Knowledge Creation refers to employee growth through performing work-related tasks, general professional experiences, and corporate training.

» Knowledge Retention is the process of permanently storing this knowledge within documents, social media platforms, and the company's internal consciousness.

» Knowledge Distribution is the transfer of knowledge from one employee to another via training, mentoring, webinars, videos, and instructional documentation.

» Mentoring your staff provides them with the opportunity to learn from your wisdom, experience, mistakes, and general insights.

» Internal company peer groups can motivate, train, and retain your best employees.

PART 3

STRUCTURING YOUR PRODUCTIVITY APPROACH

14. OPERATIONALIZING THE PYRAMID

The Productivity Pyramid System, described in detail in this chapter, is not a list of specific productivity enhancing tasks to perform. Rather, it's a framework, through which you can define and develop a successful productivity improvement process. The rationale behind this system is that organizational efficiency is best enhanced via a process that is:

» Aligned with overall organizational goals and objectives

» Able to produce real dollar savings, not just paper-based efficiencies

» Capable of increasing the Return on Investment (ROI) of existing internal resources through their reuse in innovative ways

» Designed to track the reinvestment of the time, money, and resources gained through the productivity enhancement process

To truly be effective, productivity must be viewed holistically. That is to say, in a way that considers organizational goals, internal culture, and the interaction between multiple productivity initiates.

Organizational goals: The selected productivity initiates must

> *"To truly be effective, productivity must be viewed holistically. That is to say, in a way that considers organizational goals, internal culture, and the interaction between multiple productivity initiates."*

either make it easier to achieve stated business goals, or free up existing time, money, and resources that can be directly used to support goal attainment.

Corporate culture: Like all projects, the selected productivity initiatives must be consistent with organizational values and performed in a way that takes advantage of organizational strengths and avoids weaknesses.

Project interaction: Efforts to improve productivity in one area can stymie efforts in other areas. For example, an initiative to reduce the number of meetings makes it more difficult to enhance the efficiency of existing business processes. Another example, the reduction of emails may cause the need for additional meetings. Also, enhancing the efficiency of a process that will be phased out due to the implementation of a corporate goal negates its return on investment.

This seven step process moves you from the initial analysis of your organizational goals, through project definition, selection and execution, to the capture and reinvestment of harvested savings.

Remember from Chapter 4, the Productivity Pyramid System contains the following steps as seen in Figure 1:

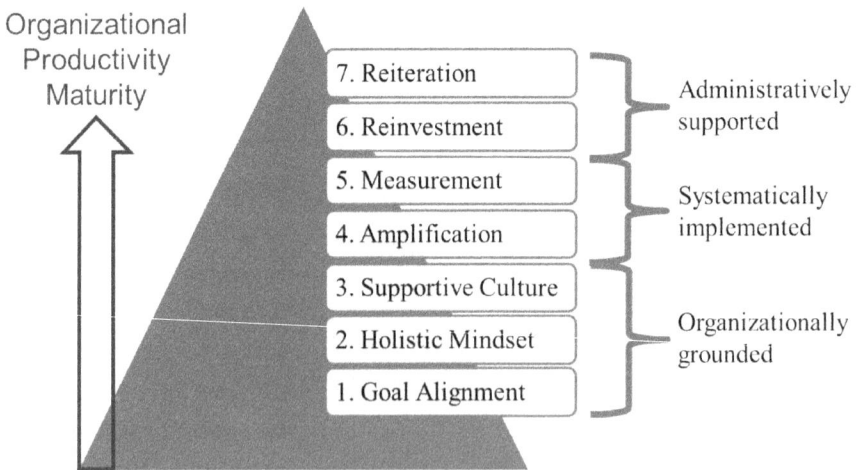

(Figure 1)

Figure 1 illustrates seven key factors that are required maximize organizational productivity:

While this process is primarily used to define and execute productivity related projects, it has the additional benefit of enhancing the probability of success of non-productivity related projects. For example, if you are replacing your accounting system because your old vendor is phasing out the product, then the Productivity Enabler analysis can help you identify cultural issues that will affect the ease or difficulty related to introducing the system to those working in the accounting department. Another example, you may find that enhancing internal knowledge transfer may have the indirect benefit of reducing attrition because employees feel that the additional knowledge they are gaining is expanding their professional marketability.

1. Goal Alignment

Understanding organizational goals should be the basis for expenditures and activities of all types, including productivity initiatives. Aligning your improvement projects with corporate goals not only provides longer lasting benefits, but also makes it easier for you to get project funding. The benefits are longer lasting, because they are in areas the company is moving toward, not away.

If you are overseeing the productivity initiatives of the entire corporate entity, the organization's overall goals should be used. If you are leading the productivity effort of an organizational sub-group, such as IT, HR or Sales, then you must also include the goals of your specific business sub-group. In addition to making good business sense, it will also help you get your project funded.

2. Holistic Mindset

With your organizational goals in place, your next steps are to identify potential areas of improvement, define potential remedies, and create Productivity Project Definitions as a means of project approval and funding. The next three steps to do so are listed below:

1. Identify existing productivity issues that inhibit goal attainment

This step is very crucial and much easier said than done. This is where you take an honest unpolitical look at your organization, looking for present and future redundancies, inefficiencies, and process bottlenecks. Present, as you may expect, refers to issues that currently exist within the organization. Future refers to anticipated issues based on the combination of executive experience, economic forecasts and organizational direction/goals. Note that this is not the "how" things should be fixed, it's simply the identification of areas that need, or will need attention.

2. Identify needed productivity enhancements

Based on the information collected in Step #1, the next step is to define which types of productivity enhancements are required. It's best to do this all at once, versus as individual productivity issues are identified, so you can see trends, inconsistencies, and commonly needed improvements. For example, if multiple parts of the organization are saying they don't have enough time to complete their work because they spend all their time in meetings and writing emails, then a company-wide email and meeting initiative may be called for. Alternatively, if one area believes that its increasing volume is stretching its resources and other groups have excess capacity, the combination of reallocating staff and process redesign within the overworked department may be the best plan of action.

3. Convert needs into project definitions

In this step, you must transform your project ideas defined in Step #2 into high level project definitions used as the basis for approval, prioritization, and funding.

The following topics should be included in each Productivity Project Definition:

» Project Name.

» Description of the productivity issue.

» Critical Success Factors (CSFs) that will be used to measure project success.

» Expected Productivity Gains (EPGs).

» Estimated resources required.

» Estimated dollar cost.

» Known project constraints.

» Known project risks.

» Milestones.

» Timing.

The CSFs will ultimately be used to assess the project's overall success and the EPGs will be used as the basis for Productivity Driven Reinvestment, discussed later in this methodology. Remember, that CSFs and EPGs were previously described in Chapter 4.

The workbook contains worksheets that can assist you in defining your CSFs, EPGs, and their associated measurements.

These remaining Steps (#3 through #7) should only be performed on approved productivity project initiatives.

3. SUPPORTIVE CULTURE

This step assesses the organization's cultural characteristics defined earlier in the book related to the productivity project being analyzed. These cultural attributes, named "Productivity Enablers" are:

» Cultural Awareness.

» Innovative Mindset.

» Management Focus.

» Employee Communication.

» Self and Organizational Learning.

» Conflict Avoidance and Resolution.

The output of this analysis will give you help to define your project plan in regard to needed cultural change, stakeholder reporting, needed employee training, and rollout speed and process.

The accompanying workbook contains a worksheet that lists the project names on the left, each of the Productivity Enablers listed across the top and a Total Score column on the right. The process is used to assess how difficult a particular productivity project would be to implement based on cultural factors.

4. AMPLIFICATION:

This next step selects and implements the appropriate "Productivity Amplifiers" for the project described earlier within the book. These amplifiers represent eight general categories of productivity improvement. They are:

» Constructive delegation.

» Ongoing process improvement.

» Communication efficiency.

» Knowledge storage and transfer.

» Time management.

» Asset reuse.

» Intelligent meeting management.

» Leveraging the zone.

When doing the analysis of which amplifiers are applicable to the project, feel free to add additional categories as needed, based on your specific industry, company, and business situation.

Similar to the Productivity Enablers, the accompanying workbook contains a worksheet that lists the project names on the left, each of the Productivity Amplifiers listed across the middle and a Total Score column on the right.

This worksheet is designed to be used in two ways: firstly, it provides insight into which of the eight Productivity Amplifiers would be of value to the project. Secondly, there is a total at the bottom of each Amplifier column, which provides insights into which of the Amplifiers are most important overall. Therefore, if enhanced, would be of value to the maximum number of projects. For example, if a large number of business areas state that knowledge transfer from older to younger employees was an issue, then enhance the organization's overall knowledge transfer related abilities could provide value throughout the organization.

Regarding project implementation, the project management process is a book unto itself. So for now, I'll simply say remember to follow best practices, give credit to those who deserve it, celebrate small successes to build momentum, provide continued status reporting to your stakeholders, and have a little fun along the way.

Remember, project success is one of the best ways to illustrate your leadership ability and measureable productivity gains are the steppingstones to the approval of future productivity initiatives.

> "Project success is one of the best ways to illustrate your leadership ability and measureable productivity gains are the steppingstones to the approval of future productivity initiatives."

5. MEASUREMENT

With the productivity project Critical Success Factors (CSFs) and Expected Productivity Gains (EPGs) measurements defined and the project completed, the next step will properly measure the project's productivity gains. These gains should be categorized as specifically defined within the Productivity Project Definition:

» Direct cash savings.

» Time saving of hourly employees and contractors resulting in cash savings.

» Freeing up of non-cash resources (such as computer equipment, office space, and etc.).

» Time savings of salaried employees that reduce full time staff needs that can be redeployed.

» Time savings of salaried employees that can be specifically redirected to other tasks.

» Time savings of salaried employees that cannot be specifically redirected to other tasks.

When reviewing the above list of measurements, you will see that they can loosely be divided into the following three types:

1. CSFs within the Productivity Project Definition, used to assess project success.

2. Savings that are good to know and are of value, but are not directly reusable

3. EPGs within the Productivity Project Definition and other recapturable savings to be used in the next step (Productivity Driven Reinvestment).

The last category listed above will be the basis for the Productivity Driven Reinvestment discussed in the next section.

6. PRODUCTIVITY DRIVEN REINVESTMENT

This step is the capture and reinvestment of your productivity gains. In many ways, this is the most important part of the process. This newfound time, money, and resource can be used to fund new projects, increase operating income, enhance client service, and /or create new revenue streams.

The key is to keep track of how they are used. All too often, the day after the project ends, people are moved to the next project and

everything associated with the old
project is forgotten. The workbook
associated with this book contains
worksheets that can assist you in
tracking the usage of these newly
found corporate assets.

> *"The key is to keep track of how this new time, money, and resources are used."*

At the end of the day, people aren't interested in time management, process improvement, or any of the other productivity amplifiers. They are also not even really interested in the productivity these activities create. The thing corporate executives are most interested in is the opportunity that productivity provides.

7. REITERATIVE

This last step is the key to maintaining the ongoing momentum of your productivity improvement. Without it, organized continues improvement, as a formal business program, will cease to exist through a lack of management focus and the resulting loss of internal funding to support it. To prevent this situation from happening, at the end of each productivity project, you should have two ending "Lessons Learned" meetings.

The first meeting should be attended by key project stakeholders to gain an understanding of their perception of the project and the results it attained by asking the following questions:

» Do you believe the project was a success? Why or why not?

» From your perspective, what productivity gains were achieved?

» How will/was the time, money and resources gained by this project be used?

» In our next productivity project:

  › What should we continue to do?

  › What should we do differently?

- › What should we stop doing?
- › What should we start doing?

The second meeting should include all those that worked on the project. It should be with a debriefing from the first meeting and then ask the following questions:

- » In our next productivity project:
  - › What should we continue to do?
  - › What should we do differently?
  - › What should we stop doing?
  - › What should we start doing?
- » What, if anything, should we do differently based on the feedback from the stakeholder meeting?
- » Do you think additional efficiencies could have been gained via this project? If yes, how?
- » What else can we do in our next productivity project to:
  - › Harvest additional time, money and resources?
  - › Reduce project stress?
  - › Have more fun?

With these questions answered and your next productivity approved, you should take advantage of the momentum you have earned, maybe a little bit of the time, money, and resources you have recovered, and the lessons you have learned to continue enhancing your organizational efficiency.

As time passes and you look back at the multiple productivity projects you have led, like sands in an hourglass, their collective organizational efficiencies have truly helped move your organization and your career forward.

15. PRODUCTIVITY LINKING AND MAPPING

Every department within an organization is part of an overall ecosystem and is connected to all other departments in some way. For example, Human Resources (HR) helps hire staff in Information Technology (IT), Sales, Warehousing and Finance. IT maintains the systems used by the HR, Sales, Warehousing and Finance. The Sales team sells the product. Warehousing ships the product to the customer. Accounts Receivable sends an invoice to the customer and processes the incoming payment. If any of these departments fall short in the execution of their responsibilities, then the company could fail. As a result of this interrelationship, productivity initiatives in any one department can positively affect other areas of the company. This concept is called "Productivity Linking". Understanding these connections allows you to strategically prioritize your productivity initiatives, based on what is best for the company as a whole.

> *"Productivity Linking is defining the productivity connections between departments. Productivity Mapping is the process of defining this linkage."*

The technique used to document and analyze these connects is called "Productivity Mapping".

The Productivity Mapping process begins by defining your primary goal. These goals loosely fall into three fundamental categories.

1. General Productivity Enhancement

2. Specific Department Productivity Enhancement

3. Specific Process Productivity Enhancement

General Productivity Enhancement is the goal of enhancing the organization's overall efficiency toward the attainment of corporate-level goals. These goals could be increased profitability, corporate growth or increasing the funding to key activities such as marketing or product research and development. If this is your goal, follow these steps:

1. IDENTIFY AND DOCUMENT DEPARTMENTAL DEPENDENCIES

Establishing department dependencies back to their original source allows you to maximize the benefits of your productivity investment by starting at the root sources of your department and working your way forward. At a very high organizational level, the Product Map may look like this:

General Productivity Enhancement Map

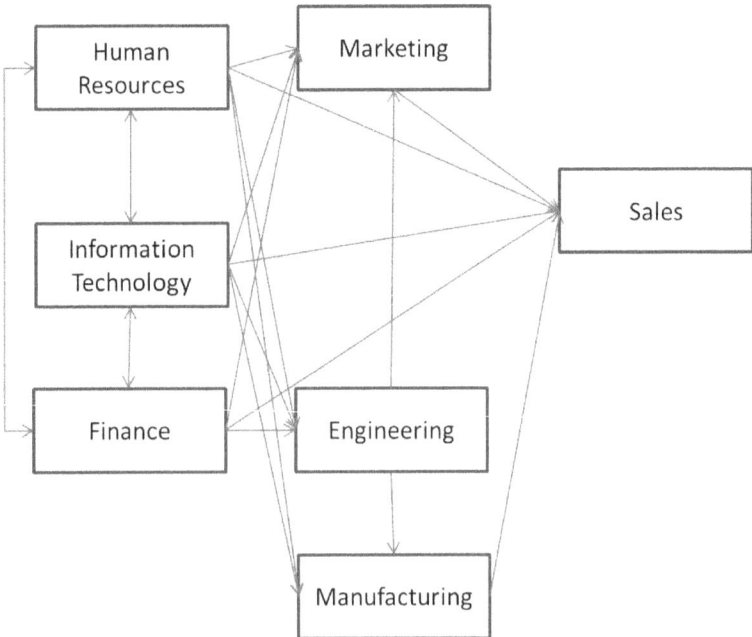

Given the above Productivity Map, logic would dictate that you first enhance the efficiency of HR, IT and Finance, because enhanced efficiencies in these areas will provide value to the organizations they serve, namely Marketing, Engineering, Manufacturing and Sales. This may seem counter-intuitive to think that the first step to improving Marketing's efficiency is to enhance HR, IT and Finance, but if inefficiencies in these three groups are truly hurting Marketing's efficiency it may be the best place to start.

Note that your department analysis should not stop at the functional level, such as IT or HR. For example, within IT, the Help Desk assists employees company-wide, including employees within IT itself. As a second example, the IT group that supports the financial systems only provides assistance to the Finance group.

2. BEGIN YOUR PRODUCTIVITY INITIATIVES AT THE ROOT SOURCE DEPARTMENTS

When performing this type of analysis, you will most likely see that the internal service organizations, such as IT, Human Resources and Finance provide support to all parts of the organization (including each other). As a result, enhancing the productivity of these three areas first, allows them to better serve their internal clients throughout the organization. This enhanced productivity has three potential uses:

a. Reducing the cost of internal overhead functions, thus providing time, money and resources for other non-overhead based activities

b. Reinvesting the productivity gains within the overhead functions to enhance their ability to provide service throughout the company

c. Reinvesting the harvested time and resources in other productivity initiatives and use the harvested money to enhance profitability

3. MOVE STEP-BY-STEP THROUGH YOUR PRODUCTIVITY MAP TO ALL PARTS OF THE COMPANY

With your root level department productivity projects completed, move forward department-by-department, in the order identified and illustrated in your Productivity Enhancement Map, to enhance the efficiency of other departments further down the productivity chain.

Specific Department Productivity Enhancement is the goal of enhancing the efficiency of a specific department. In this case, the Productivity Map is department centric. That is to say, you map its

a. Organizational dependencies

b. Incoming process dependencies

c. Internal department processes

d. Required output

The high level Productivity Map illustrating this concept is shown below.

Specific Department Productivity Enhancement

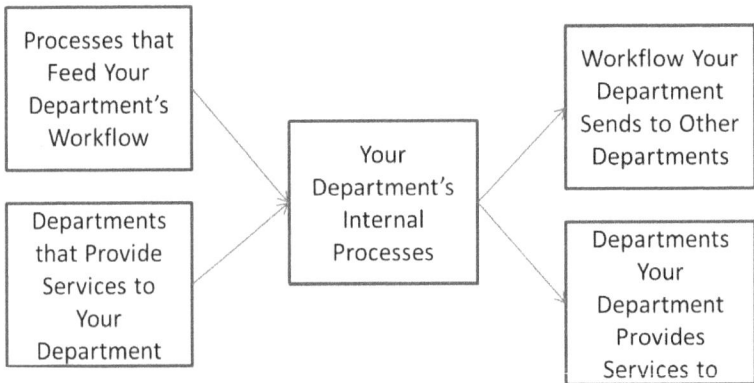

The steps related to department level productivity enhancements are:

1. Build your department's Productivity Map
2. Define how your department's productivity can be enhanced via the groups providing your department workflow and/or support in some manner
3. Meet with the managers of these supporting departments with the goal of enhancing and/or modifying the service your group is being provided
4. Analyze the services you are providing to others and internal services you perform for internal consumption
5. Prioritize your internal department processes based on the analysis performed within step #4

Specific Process Productivity Enhancement is the goal of enhancing a specific company or department-specific process. Using the Sales area as an example, you may have the following process:

a. Sales Research looks for potential customers to call
b. Call Center makes outbound cold calls based on sales research lists
c. Sales Professionals follow up on Call Center leads

The Productivity Map for this scenario is shown below.

Specific Process Productivity Enhancement

| Sales Research | → | Call Center | → | Sales Professionals |

The steps for enhancing a single process can be performed using any number of standard process reengineering techniques that your organization may already be deploying. At high level, I would suggest the following:

1. Build a process Productivity Map

2. When analyzing the map, if there are any clear bottlenecks in the process, correct those first

3. If you are simply trying to enhance the process's overall output and/or efficiency, consider the following:

    a. If you start at its root activity and then move forward, based on the maximum capacity of downstream processes, you may be creating downstream bottlenecks

    b. If you start at the last step and move backward through the process, it may be a long time before you reap the benefits of enhanced efficiencies

    c. The direction you go (start-to-finish or end-to-start) should be based on the type of process being enhanced and the ramifications related to feeding more volume into the pipeline that can't be promptly served.

KEY CHAPTER TAKEAWAYS

» Productivity Linking is defining the productivity connections between departments.

» Productivity Mapping the process of defining this linkage

» There are three primary types of productivity goals.

  › General Productivity Enhancement

  › Specific Department Productivity Enhancement

  › Specific Process Productivity Enhancement

16. GETTING YOUR PRODUCTIVITY PROJECTS FUNDED

The best project proposals in the world can't provide value to your organization if they don't get funded. Therefore, part of your productivity initiative must be a strategy to get your projects approved, and properly resourced. Should you be a senior executive and in the position to fund these types of projects, if:

» You think they make good business sense.

» Internal resources exist that can be invested in productivity improvement.

» They can free up time, money and/or resources that can be used in other ways.

» They can assist in the attainment of current organizational goals.

» The efficiencies they provide will be of value once current goals are attained.

Then simply make the decision to move forward, if it is within your power to do so. However, if you are not a decision maker in your organization's project approval process, then this chapter is for you.

Creating a quality project proposal (also often called Project Scope Documents) is only the beginning. Getting it approved, prioritized, and funded is a whole different story.

There are a number of basic techniques you can use to help you get all projects funded, they are:

- » Aligning your project with a specific organizational goal.
- » Aligning your project to a large internal initiative that already has funding.
- » Choosing an inspiring project name.
- » Find an executive sponsor to help you justify and prioritize your project.
- » Clearly describe how the benefits outweigh the costs.
- » Form internal alliances as soon as possible with people who believe that your project will be of value and can help you get it approved.
- » Avoid organizational, political, and technical complexities.
- » Quickly and effectively answer your critics, don't leave today's issue until tomorrow.
- » Get excited about the project yourself, excitement is infectious.

There are also a number of techniques you can employ specifically designed to get productivity-related projects approved and prioritized. They are:

> *"There are also a number of techniques you can employ specifically designed to get productivity-related projects approved and prioritized."*

CLEAR ARTICULATION OF THE BENEFITS

Clearly articulate how the regained time, money, and resources will be used to benefit the organization. This is a nice way of describing the current lost opportunity cost of inefficient operations. Remember to emphasize real dollar savings versus small bits of time saved by salaried employees. The latter will be discounted as non-retrievable unless you can illustrate how this gained time will be used for business gain.

CONSIDER SAVINGS FROM RELATED PROJECTS

If appropriate, quantify the added savings that can be achieved based upon the completion of other major initiatives. For example, if a new accounting system is being installed and your productivity project will have increased value to the organization after the new system is implemented, then include it in your savings calculations. This has two benefits: firstly, it props up your project savings. Secondly, the people involved in the accounting system project will become allies because your project will enhance the value of their project.

FIND MULTIPLE SOURCES OF PROJECT FUNDING

If your project is cross-functional in nature, such as reducing the number of meetings or the reuse of assets, then try to get multiple business areas to sponsor/fund your project. This approach minimizes the budget impact on any one organizational area.

BE POLITICALLY ASTUTE

Gain a deep understanding of the political impact of your project. Many productivity projects -by their nature- cause change. As a result, they may be perceived as winners or losers. An understanding of these dynamics will help avoid political landmines and help cultivate potential project sponsors.

With your productivity project well positioned, your next step is to submit your proposal through your organization's standard approval process. This may seem like an obvious thing to do, but historically, productivity, and quality related projects all too often were able to bypass the standard funding process. This was the case because a high ranking executive pushed it through the system due do his/her strength of personality and purpose. While these types of projects were able to move ahead quickly, their entire future was tied to the executive that sponsored it. As a result, when this executive left the company, changed internal roles simply fell from grace, the person's "pet" productivity projects were defunded and quickly disappeared.

The advantage of following the organization's traditional/standard approval process is that it moves your productivity-related projects into the mainstream; therefore, the removal of a single executive will not jeopardize the project's approval, prioritization, funding, staffing, or other similar activities. In essence, it saves your project from being viewed as a "side project" always struggling for resources and legitimacy.

Once it's approved, then congratulations are given, the project team is formed, and the work begins.

PART 4

PRODUCTIVITY SUPERSTARS

17. CEO HAS THINNING PROFIT MARGINS

_____

Michael, the CEO of a $100 million consulting company, was proud to tell his customers, friends, and family that his company had a 25% year over year growth. The issue he kept highly confidential was that his company's expenses were growing by 33% a year. His company was profitable, but this trend could not continue indefinitely.

To make matters worse, Michael had aspirations of taking his company public. However to do so, he must first prove that his company's business model can show economies of scale and increases, versus decrease in profit margin as the company sales grow. To solve this dilemma, Michael brought in various consultants and had limited success. His friend, Justin Tyme, told him about a productivity methodology he had heard about called the Productivity Pyramid System (PPS). Michael told Justin that at this point, he would try anything to raise his profit margins.

Michael scheduled a meeting with his senior management team to discuss the issue. He begin the having a consultant describe the PPS process and the eight Productivity Amplifiers.

Wanting to follow the PPS process, Michael began the meeting by outlining the following business goals:

1. We must find a way to increase sales in a way that does not deteriorate our profit margins.

2. We need to increase our investment in new product development, partially funded via the time, money, and resource gains created by this productivity initiative.

Also, understanding that his company's corporate culture may have contributed to some of the inefficiencies within his organization, he assured his staff that the reported inefficiencies would not be viewed as poor previous leadership. He said that to the contrary, the willingness of those on his team to bring forward innovative ideas to enhance efficiency will be rewarded. He also said that those in the room should treat the people on their teams with the same courtesy.

Michael then went on to say that each proposed project must have defined and measurable productivity gains. Also, these gains must be real savings, such as lower transaction costs, reduced headcount, lower vendor costs, or other real dollar savings. They must be real dollars, not "funny money" savings related to potential twenty or thirty minute productivity gains for salaried employees, unless they can definitively illustrate how and where these productivity gains will be recaptured for the company's benefit.

Then, Michael instructed his leadership team to return to their groups, identify opportunities for operational efficiencies, create project proposals, and return in one month for project approval and prioritization.

Four weeks passed and Michael's executive team reconvened to continue their productivity enhancement discussion.

The VP of Sales, Wanda Moremoney, said she could reduce the cost of sales by bringing one less person on each sales meeting. She said that she assessed the cost of each sales call based on their travel expenses and the approximate hourly salary of each employee attending the meetings. She went on to say, that the travel expenses will save approximately $1,250 per sales call and the time savings would be used to increase the number of outbound sales calls and visits per week. This may not sound like much, however, given that there are approximately 20 sales calls per month, that's an annual savings of $300,000 plus one full headcount that can move from sales visits to outbound sales calls.

The VP of Marketing, Crystal Ball, and the head of training, Will Teachum, realized that if they worked together they could reduce the cost of both marketing collateral and training materials by repurposing each other's existing written content. Of course, there were differences in what they needed, but using each other's materials as a base would be much less costly than developing them from scratch. Crystal went on to say he was also analyzing their social media processes and policies to see if money and/or time could be saved, but that this analysis would take an additional two or three weeks to complete.

The VP of Human Resources, Ivana Goodday, said she hadn't realized how much time her staff was spending writing emails. She said that reducing the amount of time her group spent writing emails would not have a direct cash benefit, but suggested that it would allow her team to spend more time recruiting quality candidates, dealing with employee issues, and streamlining the employee performance review process which would benefit managers throughout the company.

The VP of Information Technology, Rusty Steel, who was very excited about this project since its inception, said that he combined time management, meeting reductions, and constructive delegation. He said that he believes that productivity gained by implementing these concepts will allow him to hold his team's headcount flat; therefore, not needing the seven additions to headcount that had previously been approved. This headcount reduction would have an annual savings of approximately $850,000.

Guy Numbers, the CFO, said that there was also some inefficiency within his department. He told Michael that because the company has grown so fast, the internal financial processes have not been able to keep up with it. As a result, the cost per transaction could be dramatically reduced through automation with the help of Rusty Steel's IT team. An added benefit of this automation is that if they can bill the clients more efficiently, then they may be able to shorten the number of collection days which would be of great value to the overall cash flow.

Lastly, the Operations Manager, Patti O'Furniture, looked down at the conference table and said he believed that a major portion of the reduced margin was based on inefficiencies within warehouse operations and product shipping. As product volumes have increased, the shipping time has been extended. This caused a dramatic increase in shipping costs because more packages had to be mailed using overnight express, versus less expensive standard shipping rates. Patti went on to say that he knew more packages were being expedited in that way, but had no idea that the overall costs were so high until he analyzed his department's processes as requested the previous month.

Michael approved the proposed projects and then prioritized them based on their ability to free up needed time, money, resources and help ensure the success of future corporate initiatives.

18. AFTER YEARS OF IT BUDGET CUTS, CIO GETS GROWTH

After years of being told to cut his budget, the CIO, Kerry Oki, was very happy to receive the news from his boss that the IT budget would be expanding by 5% in the upcoming year. He was excited about his new initiatives he wanted to fund; however, that 5% he was given wasn't enough to fund his cloud computing and mobility based initiatives.

Kerry spoke with the head of his Project Management Office (PMO), Sandy Beach, and asked if he knew of any productivity tools that help stretch the IT budget. Sandy told Kerry that he had to just read Eric Bloom's new book on productivity and it contained an interesting new methodology called the Productivity Pyramid System (PPS). It starts by looking at the overall organizational goals: in their case, corporate and IT goals. Then it tries to identify inefficiencies, assess organizational culture based on six Productivity Enablers, and categorizes corrective action based on eight Productivity Amplifiers. Kerry didn't really understand what Sandy was talking about, but said it sounded interesting and wanted to try it as a test case within the Software Development Group.

Sandy looked through the Productivity Amplifiers and decided that instead of using the PPS methodology as designed, he was very intrigued by the idea of "Asset Reuse" and thought he would look for places within the Software Development group to give it a try. He set up a meeting with Stanley Cupp, the VP of Software Development. During their discussion they identified three potential Asset Reuse candidates.

The first potential candidate was allowing the Software Testing group to store their regression test cases in the source code control software used by the programmers. The second potential candidate was allowing the Internal Customer Service group to use the remote PC control software used by the Help Desk to access user desktops. The third potential reuse candidate was allowing the rest of the company to use their corporate license of Microsoft Project for non-IT related projects. This third potential reuse won't save money within IT, but it provides the company, in general, with a great new software tool at no additional cost. This is definitely a win for the company and a win for IT.

Kerry told Sandy he was very impressed that he was able to find three quality opportunities so quickly. He then asked him to consider ways that the other seven Productivity Amplifiers could be used with IT and the company in general. He also instructed Sandy to further investigate the PPS process as a standard methodology to be used with the PMO.

19. SVP OF SALES HIRES A CONSULTANT

Kelly Green, the SVP of Sales, led a great sales organization with 85% of her salesforce consistently exceeding their annual sales quotas. Her issue was that the sales support groups were having trouble keeping up with ever increasing sales volumes. These groups included Order Entry, Contract Writing, and Post-Sales Support. On one hand, she would smile and say that having trouble processing so many incoming orders was a good problem to have. On the other hand, she recognized that it was a very serious business issue because it gave a bad first impression to new customers, slowed incoming cash flow, and occasionally sales were cancelled due to customer frustration.

The issue of these processing delays came to light when a major client called Kelly and said that if they couldn't improve their order processing and post-sales support, then they would stop buying products from the company.

This customer call became a turning point in Kelly's thinking. Instead of seeing these delays as simply a frustration, she was now seeing them as a major sales issue and wanted it corrected as soon as possible. She didn't believe the issue was related to department size because she was continually adding staff as sales volumes increased.

Kelly asked Joe Technica, a consultant that she had hired over the years, to help her with organizational issues and process automation. After signing a Non-Disclosure Agreement, agreeing on a consulting rate, and a quick analysis of the three struggling groups (Order Entry,

Contract Writing and Post-Sales Support), Joe said that it was a classic case of very good people, antiquated processes, and poor productivity practices. He went on to suggest that Kelly use the Productivity Pyramid System (PPS) to enhance their organizational efficiency.

Kelly said it sounded like a funny name for productivity methodology, but agreed, Joe's contract was extended and work began.

Since Joe proposed using PPS, he decided to follow it exactly. He felt that not only would it give structure to the consulting engagement and get the job done; in addition, it would also provide him the opportunity to give Kelly ongoing deliverables, show his progress as he moved from step to step, and gain a deeper understanding of Kelly's overall organization with the hope of gaining additional consulting work.

1. GOAL ALIGNMENT

Joe began by asking Kelly for the company's overall goals for the year ahead, her organizational goals, and those of each of the three departments to be analyzed. He went on to say that these were a vital part of the process because all proposed productivity enhancements should be directly in line with organizational and departmental goals. He said that all suggested future productivity initiatives either increase the probability of meeting these defined goals or provide time, money, and/or resources that can be put toward goal related projects.

2. HOLISTIC MINDSET

After analyzing the organization's goals, Joe's next step was to do the following:

1. Identify existing productivity issues.
2. Identify needed productivity enhancements.
3. Convert needs into project definitions.
4. Complete a Productivity Project/Enabler Matrix.

5. Complete a Productivity Project/Amplifier Matrix.

Joe really liked this step in the methodology because it allowed him the opportunity to truly analyze what was needed (#1 and #2), before having to make specific project recommendations in a later step. This step provided him with important knowledge needed to truly provide value to his client.

3. SUPPORTIVE CULTURE

One single productivity improvement project was selected as the test case.

With his test project in hand, Joe's next step was to analyze the organization's culture based on the six Productivity Enablers and their effect on the project. The six productivity enablers are:

» Cultural Awareness.

» Innovative Mindset.

» Management Focus.

» Employee Communication.

» Self and Organizational Learning.

» Conflict Avoidance and Resolution.

As a consultant, Joe wasn't generally interested in corporate culture. He just liked to figuratively come in on his shining white horse, discover the problem, define the solution, save the day, and ride into the sunset as a hero. However in this case, he was very glad that PPS had a cultural component. Upon analysis, he realized their productivity issues were primarily caused by a lack of management focus and poor employee communication.

4. AMPLIFICATION

Joe thought to himself that this was his favorite part of the PPS process because this is where he gets to define the solutions, based on the issues defined in Step 2 (Holistic Mindset) and the cultural landscape defined in Step 3 (Supportive Culture).

Given the nature of the project and his understanding of the cultural issues, Joe made the decision that if he could not get the VP of Sales and his senior staff to concentrate on the project, then he would step away from it versus see it fail. Because he had previously worked with Kelly Green, he didn't think that this would be the case, so he decided to cautiously move forward.

Knowing that improvements in one Productivity Amplifier can sometimes be offset by losses in others; Joe decided that process improvement was the overlying objective and have all other amplifiers, for now, fall as they may. This approach reminded him of a quote by President Dwight D. Eisenhower: "We succeed only as we identify in life, or in war, or in anything else, a single overriding objective, and make all other considerations bend to that one objective." Joe smiled and thought that if this concept was good enough for President Eisenhower, it was good enough for him.

As a result of taking this approach, he recommended the following plan of action:

1. Create a Sales Process Improvement Team (SPIT), including senior representatives of the Sales, Order Entry, Contract Writing, and Post-Sales Support groups.

2. Assign SPIT the responsibility to:

    a. Analyze and document the existing sales processes.

    b. Make recommendations on how to streamline these processes.

    c. The representatives of each group will then lead the implementation of the team's suggestions within their respective groups.

As part of this process, Joe also instructed the SPIT members to do the following as part of their analysis:

» Include a representative of the Information Technology (IT) group. They can provide input as to how technology can be used to enhance the sales processes.

» While analyzing the core sales processes for potential efficiency improvements, take note of the other Productivity Amplifiers for future secondary productivity improvements. In particular, look for:

› Sales processes, tools, and technologies that can be used in other ways.

› Meetings and committees that are no longer needed, have too many attendees, or meet too often given the value they provide.

› Management-level bottlenecks that could be removed though better delegation.

› Communication efficiencies between the various SPIT group members to facilitate continued process improvements.

With his instructions given and the SPIT team formed, Joe's next tasks were to facilitate their meetings, assist the SPIT representatives implement process change within their respective business areas, put processes in place to collect the needed statistics to measure the process improvements, and track freed up time, money, and resources for future redeployment.

5. MEASUREMENT

With the processes redesigned and in use, Joe moved the SPIT meetings from weekly to monthly. He decided it was best to keep the team together because the lack of communication across the various sales groups contributed to the poor processes that had previously been in use.

Joe also was perfectly positioned to begin collecting the results of the improved processes. These measurements, initially defined in Step

2 (Holistic Mindset) and operationalized in Step 4 (Amplification), were now starting to show the gains resulting from their productivity efforts.

What they learned from these measurements was that having the order entry, contract writing, and post-sales support processes streamlined and more coordinated had two benefits: firstly, they were better able to bring on new customers more efficiently. Secondly, they were able to free up one order entry person and three post-sales people by removing redundant processes. It also reduced the need for as much travel to the customer's site, reducing travel costs, and the need for local contractors. These financial savings were estimated at approximately $25,000 per month. To Kelly Green, freeing up four people and saving $300,000 a year was nice, but the real win was the improvements made to the sales process.

6. PRODUCTIVITY DRIVEN REINVESTMENT

Remembering Joe's comment about primary and secondary objectives, Kelly Green felt that his first objective of streamlining inefficient sales processes is well underway. With that in place, Kelly thanked Joe for his outstanding work and asked him to perform one additional task. This task was to perform a quick analysis as to where the four freed up resources and $300,000 annual savings could be used to further enhance overall sales efficiency and effectiveness.

7. REITERATIVE

To help continue the ongoing productivity improvement momentum, following the PPS methodology, Joe led two final meetings. The first meeting was with the project stakeholders, which included Kelly and the SPIT members, to get their perspective on how the project was run and its ultimate results. The second meeting was with those who worked on the project to gain their thoughts about future project on:

» What they should continue to do?

» What they should do differently?

» What they should stop doing?

» What they should start doing?

To close out his consulting engagement correctly, Joe documented his work, including the notes from the two debriefing meetings, with two purposes in mind. First, and foremost, was to provide Kelly Green with a blueprint of how PPS was used to enhance her team's productivity so it could be used again on future productivity related projects. This documentation included a list of secondary productivity enhancement projects that were uncovered and put on hold during the Amplification phase.

Second, as a consultant, Joe wanted to leave Kelly with an ending deliverable that outlined what was done and potential follow-up assignments as a reference document for Kelly and as a subtle marketing tool for himself. Joe produced great results and hoped to be called upon again to help Kelly and/or to provide assistance in other parts of the company.

20. SVP OF HUMAN RESOURCES LEADS THE CHARGE

The SVP of Human resources (HR), Ivana Goodday, was asked by the company president to lead a company-wide effort to enhance employee productivity.

Having looked at various productivity-related processes, practices and methodologies, Ivana decided to move forward with the principles in a class by Manager Mechanics taken by two of her staff members. The class was named "Productivity Driven Success". This class took a holistic view of organizational productivity. In particular, she liked the concepts of Productivity Enablers, which related to organizational culture and the Productivity Amplifiers, which are eight ways to enhance organizational efficiency. It was also the first time she had seen the concept of the "Productivity Measurement Fallacy" and the idea that if not viewed holistically improving productivity of one activity can adversely affect productivity in another one. In particular, she liked the example that reducing email can create the need for more meetings. These types of real life examples within the class made her feel that the topics within it were based on reality, not conjecture.

She was also impressed with the Productivity Pyramid, which started with an understanding of corporate goals and ended with a measurable and repeatable process. She thought it would help the company in the short term as well as long into the future. At a personal level, she also liked the idea of heading up this project because she saw it as an interesting professional challenge and an expansion of her current role within the company.

Given her company-wide viewpoint and background in Human resources, she decided to begin by devising a plan to create an internal company culture of continuous improvement based on the six Productivity Enablers outlined within the class. This list of enablers was:

1. Cultural Awareness.
2. Innovative Mindset.
3. Management Focus.
4. Employee Communication.
5. Self and Organizational Learning.
6. Conflict Avoidance and Resolution.

While she agreed with the class authors that these six enablers made very good sense from a productivity enhancement perspective, she also felt that these six areas would help reduce attrition, enhance employee morale, increase organizational bench strength, and foster internal organizational cooperation.

She began by asking Manager Mechanics to lead a series of custom two day workshops across the company containing concepts, processes, and best practices related specifically to the six productivity enablers. She felt that, given her HR background, it was much easier to get agreement and cooperation from those asked to implement new productivity initiatives if the right internal culture was already in place.

With the needed cultural change in process, Ivana then turned her attention to the eight Productivity Accelerators, listed below:

» Creative delegation.

» Ongoing process improvement.

» Communication efficiency.

» Knowledge storage and transfer.

» Time management.

» Asset reuse.

» Intelligent meeting management.

» Leveraging the zone.

She overheard those on her team who had taken the class talking about productivity cocktails and thought they went out for a drink after class. After closer examination of the eight Productivity Accelerators, she realized the first letter of each spells the word "cocktail". She thought that was a rather cute touch and laughed to herself because she didn't really think that Susan and Chris, who attended the class, where the drinking type.

Once again, Ivana wanted to play to her strengths, decided it would be best to initially keep away from department-level processes, and began by enhancing the productivity of general company activities. The accelerators she chose were delegation, time management, communication and meetings. Ivana was also very interested in getting involved in knowledge transfer, but thought that should come next. She also decided to select these topics because when looking at the class workbook, she thought they had some very unique and interesting concepts that would be of real value to the organization.

Ivana thought the Productivity Enablers class went well and wanted to offer all employees world-wide the opportunity to take the class on delegation, time management, communication and meetings.

With two major productivity successes behind her, she decided to team up with the head of Information Technology (IT), to tackle the process improvement and asset reuse accelerators because IT could provide great insights and be a strong internal partner on these two important activities.